Mind and Simulation

FEVZI H.

MIND AND SIMULATION

Is Our Perception of Reality an Illusion?

2025

Mind and Simulation

Fevzi H.

CONTENTS

About the Author

I am Fevzi H., a thinker and author with deep knowledge in the fields of science and philosophy, exploring multidisciplinary concepts. Questioning the boundaries between the physical and metaphysical worlds, I am on an intellectual journey to understand the universal nature of consciousness. For years, I have been researching topics such as consciousness, quantum mechanics, parallel universes, and artificial intelligence, combining scientific theories with philosophical approaches to delve deeper into the complexities of the human mind.

In my writings, I present radical ideas about the nature of consciousness and its connection to the universe. By examining not only scientific data but also the intellectual heritage of humanity, I aim to offer my readers new perspectives. My writing style revolves around simplifying complex theories and using a language that encourages deep thinking.

Each of my works invites readers to take another step toward uncovering the mysteries of the universe and consciousness. By merging modern scientific thought with philosophical inquiry, I offer innovative and thought-provoking perspectives on the nature of consciousness and its universal connections.

Foreword

The nature of reality has been one of humanity's deepest and most perplexing questions. Do we truly exist in the way we perceive, or is our experience of reality merely an illusion? Is the world presented to us by our senses a faithful representation of the truth, or is it a sophisticated simulation crafted by our brains? From ancient philosophers to modern quantum physicists, this inquiry has shaped the very foundations of our understanding.

This book brings together multiple disciplines to explore the limits of perception, consciousness, and the universe itself. Drawing from philosophy, neuroscience, quantum physics, and artificial intelligence, it delves into the mysteries of existence and the possibility that what we call "reality" might be something far more complex than we assume.

Through the lens of thinkers like Plato, Descartes, Berkeley, and Bostrom, we examine philosophical perspectives on the nature of reality and the possibility that we may be living in a simulation. At the same time, we explore the latest scientific discoveries, from the bizarre principles of quantum mechanics to the brain's ability to shape perception and the implications of artificial intelligence in creating new simulated worlds.

If we are living in a simulation, what does that mean? Is the universe a mathematical construct, governed by codes and algorithms? Is our brain not only experiencing a simulation but also generating its own? And perhaps the most intriguing question of all—if we are inside a simulation, is there any way to escape?

This book is an intellectual journey through the intersection of science, philosophy, and technology, designed for those who seek to challenge the boundaries of their understanding. Be prepared to rethink everything you know—because reality may not be as real as it seems.

CHAPTER 1

The Fundamentals of Our Perception of Reality

1.1 What is Reality? The Line Between Perception and Truth

Reality is one of the fundamental building blocks of our lives; it forms the muse upon which the whole thing rests, and it constitutes the space wherein we exist and experience the sector. However, this concept has been the concern of philosophical inquiry throughout human history. What is reality? Is reality the essence of everything, or are we simply grounded in an phantasm? These questions had been examined from both philosophical and scientific views, leading to the development of numerous viewpoints. The line among truth and perception is vital to this information.

In philosophical phrases, reality is every so often used to refer to the goal international, however it can also be defined as a assemble shaped with the aid of notion. To draw close what kind of truth we're talking approximately, we need to first clarify the meaning of the word "fact." Reality is normally understood because the lifestyles of outside items, independent of human notion. These entities are believed to exist irrespective of our recognition of them. However, does the goal interpretation of fact make clear the line among perception and fact?

The lifestyles of physical phenomena which includes the Earth, the solar system, galaxies, and the shape of the universe can be confirmed through clinical statement. These phenomena suggest the lifestyles of a world past human focus. However, the question of whether or not there's simplest one form of reality remains more complicated. Is reality an absolute time-honored construct, or is it a shape formed via the perceptions of every individual?

Perception is the closest experience we ought to truth. However, belief is a private and subjective technique. Our senses obtain facts from the external world, which is then interpreted and understood by means of the mind. But the accuracy of our notion relies upon on how our mind strategies the sensory records. In different words, the external reality is reconstructed in our minds through exclusive procedures in our mind.

Our brains not best understand the records from our senses but additionally combine it with our beyond studies, cultural information, and personal ideals. This way that one person can also enjoy truth in another way from every other because belief varies in step with every character's brain structure, emotional state, and historical past.

For instance, someone status on a crowded and noisy city road may also understand the chaos in a unique way. To them, the group can also seem like a mess and confusion, while for some other man or woman, this case would possibly just be a everyday a part of every day existence. These differences spotlight how subjective notion is and display that every people reviews reality in a completely unique way.

Truth is generally understood as an objective fact. This consists of immutable entities such as the legal guidelines of nature, mathematical truths, or standard standards that exist independently of time and area. In philosophical terms, fact refers to that which aligns with "fact"; in other words, fact conforms to fact. However, questioning the lifestyles of truth has lengthy been a topic of discussion in philosophy.

Many philosophers have argued that reality exists past human perception. Plato sought fact in the realm of ideals and recommended that the bodily global become merely a shadow of this higher fact. This angle serves as an essential place to begin for thinking the nature of fact and knowledge the constrained structure of human cognizance. According to Plato, fact existed more in the intellectual realm than in the outside international.

On the alternative hand, Descartes' well-known dictum "I assume, consequently I am" sees fact as an individual verification process. Descartes doubted the life of the bodily global but affirmed the understanding of the thoughts. This technique gives perception as a intellectual technique that permits an individual to access fact.

The line among belief and reality is important to understanding how these two standards interact and shape each different. While reality is regularly visible as a reflection of belief, truth stays a deeper idea. Human cognizance may not at once get right of entry to fact, however it makes an attempt to interpret and make experience of the external international through belief.

In this context, reality is frequently visible as an goal verification, but due to the fact people's perceptions of reality range, truth takes on a one of a kind which means for every individual. For example, a scientist would possibly carry out experiments to recognize the character of the bodily international, at the same time as an artist might also goal to express truth in sensory and aesthetic phrases. Both are trying to find truth, however each follows a unique route, and every path exhibits a unique facet of fact.

The nature of reality is a conundrum that has been addressed from each philosophical and medical viewpoints. Perception performs a key function as our closest enjoy of reality, at the same time as reality represents unchanging, customary ideas. The line between the 2 can often be thin and ambiguous. Our minds only perceive reality in a limited way, and this perception consists of a unique truth for every man or woman.

Ultimately, even as truth may remain a set life inside the outside international, belief and reality are private and societal constructs which can be continuously wondered. This process leads us towards a deeper expertise of the character of fact, both at the character and typical ranges.

1.2 The Brain and Information Processing: The Connection Between the External World and Our Mind

The mind is one of the most complex and essential organs within the human body, serving as the control middle for all cognitive capabilities, from basic existence-maintaining procedures to the most superior factors of belief, reasoning, and attention. Our know-how of the world around us isn't best a made of our sensory stories however additionally the mind's difficult capacity to process, interpret, and integrate that information.

The brain features as an exceptionally state-of-the-art data-processing device. It gets input from the outdoor world thru sensory organs—which includes the eyes, ears, nostril, and skin—which convert bodily stimuli into electrical signals that may be interpreted with the aid of the brain. The brain then tactics those signals, combines them with prior reports and reminiscences, and generates a coherent representation of fact.

The central worried device plays a important role in this method. When light enters the attention, it's miles refracted onto the retina, where specialised cells (photoreceptors) convert the light into electrical alerts. These signals tour thru the optic nerve to the visible cortex, which procedures the visual records and contributes to the creation of the image we understand. Similarly, sounds are captured by way of the ears and transformed into electric indicators which might be despatched to the auditory cortex for interpretation.

However, these sensory inputs aren't virtually transmitted of their uncooked form. The brain's interpretation of sensory statistics is prompted by means of cognitive processes including attention, expectation, emotion, and earlier understanding. This is what permits us to create a intellectual model of the arena round us, where we perceive and react to objects, people, and situations in a way that isn't simplest purposeful but also meaningful to us.

Our sensory structures offer us with important data about the external global, however the brain is responsible for making sense of this information. For instance, whilst we contact a warm item, our pores and skin detects the temperature change, and sensory neurons ship this statistics to the spinal wire, which then transmits the sign to the brain. The mind strategies this facts, compares it with preceding stories, and registers the sensation of ache. This system happens so rapidly that we often perceive it as a continuous, immediately reaction.

But notion isn't just about the raw enter we receive from our sensory organs; it's also about how the brain organizes and interprets this statistics. The brain is constantly making predictions approximately the arena based on beyond reviews. These predictions help it technique sensory information greater correctly. This phenomenon is referred to as predictive coding, and it lets in the brain to generate quick responses to the world without having to procedure every little bit of records in actual time.

For example, while we see an object approaching us, the brain makes use of its preceding information to anticipate the item's trajectory and modify our responses hence. This predictive process isn't always restricted to simple reflexes however extends to complicated cognitive capabilities, consisting of language comprehension and social interactions.

One of the maximum incredible features of the brain is its potential to combine information from special sensory modalities into a unified perception of the arena. This multisensory integration permits us to create a cohesive mental version of reality, despite the truth that the information we obtain from distinct senses is processed in separate areas of the mind.

For example, when we watch someone talk, we system the visible statistics (inclusive of lip movements) within the visual cortex and the auditory facts (such as sounds) inside the auditory cortex. The brain then integrates those resources of records to generate a perception of speech that mixes each the visual and auditory components. This integration isn't always ideal, and every now and then the mind is based more closely on one experience than any other, such as while we can nevertheless apprehend a verbal exchange in a loud surroundings by way of depending more on visible cues.

Interestingly, the mind also can integrate information from exclusive sensory modalities even when there is a discrepancy among them. This is obvious in situations wherein illusions or misperceptions occur. For example, the McGurk impact is a phenomenon in which conflicting visual and auditory stimuli (including a video of someone saying one phrase whilst the audio says some other) cause a perceptual phantasm wherein the listener hears some thing totally exclusive from what is truly being stated. This indicates how the brain may be stimulated by using the mixing of multisensory records and how the external international is formed by way of this procedure.

While sensory information provides the inspiration for our knowledge of the outside global, it is the mind's cognitive procedures that refine and organize this information into coherent stories. Cognitive tactics inclusive of interest, memory, and reasoning are concerned in how we interpret and assign meaning to the sensory inputs we receive. These approaches additionally assist the mind filter and prioritize facts, allowing us to consciousness on what's maximum relevant to our immediate enjoy.

For example, interest performs a crucial role in figuring out what facts is delivered into aware cognizance. The mind is bombarded with an awesome quantity of sensory statistics, but attention permits us to consciousness on certain factors of the environment while filtering out inappropriate stimuli. This is exemplified with the aid of the cocktail birthday party impact, in which we will recognition on one conversation in a noisy room, no matter the presence of other competing sounds. Memory also plays a key role in our creation of fact, as the brain constantly updates and refines its version of the sector based on new reports.

Reasoning and hassle-solving in addition contribute to how we perceive the sector. The mind constantly analyzes and evaluates incoming statistics, making predictions about destiny events and formulating responses. These cognitive procedures are important for adapting to a dynamic world and making selections primarily based on our information of beyond reviews.

Ultimately, the mind's processing of data results in consciousness—the subjective revel in of being aware of ourselves and the arena around us. Consciousness is a complicated phenomenon that arises from the brain's activity, in particular within the better-order cortical regions. The mind

Mind and Simulation

integrates facts from one-of-a-kind sensory modalities, emotional states, and cognitive strategies to provide a unified circulate of attention.

Despite great research, the exact nature of cognizance stays one of the most profound mysteries in science. While we've got a trendy understanding of the neural mechanisms concerned in notion and cognition, the query of ways the brain generates subjective revel in continues to be largely unanswered. This enigma has led to severa theories, ranging from the idea that attention arises from unique neural circuits to the opportunity that it can be a fundamental aspect of the universe, akin to space and time.

The mind performs a valuable function in shaping our experience of reality. Through its ability to technique and combine statistics from the external world, the brain constructs a model of the arena that we perceive as actual. However, this system is not a simple mirrored image of objective reality. The brain's interpretation of sensory facts is inspired by using cognitive procedures, prior studies, and expectancies, leading to a subjective and dynamic creation of fact.

Our belief of the world isn't always a passive reception of external stimuli, however an lively process wherein the brain constantly updates its model of the world primarily based on new information. This technique highlights the complex and interconnected nature of the relationship among the outside global, the brain, and cognizance. Understanding this courting is prime to unraveling the mysteries of belief, cognition, and the nature of truth itself.

1.3 Sensory Illusions: Does the Brain Present Us with the Truth?

Our sensory structures, which consist of sight, hearing, contact, taste, and smell, are the number one manner through which we have interaction with and apprehend the world around us. These senses permit us to understand outside stimuli, offering the uncooked records that the brain makes use of to assemble a coherent version of fact. However, sensory belief isn't usually an accurate illustration of objective fact. In fact, our brains regularly create illusions—distorted perceptions of the sector—that mission our information of what's real.

Sensory illusions occur while the mind misinterprets the facts furnished via our senses, leading to a perception that does not correspond to the actual homes of the external international. These illusions aren't surely mistakes or system defects within the sensory structures; as an alternative, they spotlight the complex approaches involved in perception and the way the mind actively constructs our enjoy of reality. Illusions monitor that our sensory structures do not passively transmit uncooked statistics to the mind however instead actively manner and interpret that statistics, frequently based on earlier studies, expectancies, and contextual statistics.

For instance, visual illusions, together with the well-known Müller-Lyer illusion, exhibit how our mind can be tricked into perceiving strains as being of different lengths, despite the fact that they are identical. The brain uses contextual cues, including the route of arrows on the ends of the lines, to infer intensity and angle, however this will lead to a distorted perception of size. Similarly, the "dress" illusion, where humans see a get dressed as both white and gold or blue and black depending on their notion, highlights how distinct people' brains can interpret the equal sensory records in massively unique methods.

The phenomenon of auditory illusions also exhibits the brain's tendency to make assumptions approximately the arena. The "shepherd's tone" is an auditory phantasm that creates the belief of an with no end in sight ascending pitch, even though the sound itself is looped and now not genuinely rising. This phantasm occurs due to the fact the mind is decoding the frequency shifts in a way that shows continuous upward motion, even if no actual trade in pitch occurs.

Our sensory systems are not perfect detectors of the world; they are instead finely tuned to system statistics in a manner that facilitates us navigate our surroundings and live on. The mind actively constructs our revel in of the arena based

Fevzi H.

totally on sensory enter, prior knowledge, and predictions. This method that our perception of fact is not an specific duplicate of the external international but a dynamic and regularly incomplete model generated by means of the mind.

The mind uses numerous mechanisms to interpret sensory facts, one in every of which is top-down processing. This refers back to the mind's use of previous knowledge, expectations, and context to interpret sensory information. For example, when we see a partially obscured item, our mind makes use of earlier enjoy to fill within the gaps and create a entire picture of the item. This technique is commonly beneficial, but it could additionally lead to mistakes or illusions when the mind's expectancies war with the real sensory enter. In the case of the Müller-Lyer phantasm, for instance, the brain's assumptions about intensity and angle result in a distorted notion of line length.

In addition to pinnacle-down processing, the brain additionally relies on backside-up processing, wherein sensory statistics is analyzed at a fundamental level earlier than being included right into a more complex belief. This is the technique by which the mind gets uncooked facts from the senses (such as colorations and shapes in visual notion) and assembles it into a significant representation of the sector. While bottom-up processing affords the muse for belief, it's far the mind's top-down processing that often shapes the final enjoy.

Examples of Sensory Illusions

1. Visual Illusions: Visual illusions are some of the most well-known examples of the way our mind can misinform us. One of the most well-known visible illusions is the Müller-Lyer illusion, wherein two strains of same length seem like exceptional lengths due to the route of the arrows at their ends. This illusion takes place due to the fact our brains interpret the strains within the context of depth and angle, leading to a distorted sense of size. Another instance is the Kanizsa triangle, wherein three pacman-like figures arranged in a particular manner create the illusion of a triangle in the center, regardless of no actual triangle being present. These sorts of illusions highlight the brain's reliance on context, earlier reviews, and expectancies in building visible perception.

2. Auditory Illusions: Auditory illusions additionally display the brain's lively function in developing our experience of sound. The Shepherd's tone is an auditory illusion in which a series of overlapping tones gives the impression of an endlessly ascending pitch, even though the actual pitch of the tones does not exchange. Another famous auditory illusion is the McGurk impact, in which mismatched visible and auditory stimuli cause a perception that does not align with both stimulus. For instance, while the video of someone announcing one syllable (e.G., "ba") is paired with the audio of a special syllable (e.G., "ga"), visitors may additionally perceive a totally different

syllable (e.G., "da"), displaying how the mind integrates visual and auditory facts in complex methods.

3. Tactile Illusions: Tactile illusions arise when our experience of contact is misled via external factors. One example is the cutaneous rabbit phantasm, in which a chain of faucets on the pores and skin in a particular pattern creates the feeling of a "rabbit" hopping throughout the skin, despite the fact that no actual motion takes place. This illusion demonstrates how the brain translates sensory input from distinct places on the pores and skin and can create perceptions of motion when they're no longer sincerely present.

4. Taste and Smell Illusions: Taste and scent are also liable to illusions. The taste of sweetness can be stimulated via the coloration of the food or drink, with research showing that people are more likely to perceive a drink as sweeter if it's miles colored red or purple, even if it incorporates no introduced sugar. Similarly, the scent of meals may be altered by using the context in which it's far skilled. For instance, a meals may odor more attractive if it's far served in a pleasing environment or while accompanied via sure flavors.

One of the key motives for sensory illusions is the mind's reliance on prediction and expectation. The brain is constantly making predictions approximately what is going to happen next, based on past stories and understanding. These predictions shape our belief of the world and permit us to make short decisions. However, whilst those predictions are incorrect, the result may be a sensory illusion.

For instance, if we are in a dark room and we pay attention a sound that we interpret as a creak, our mind would possibly are expecting that it's far someone shifting close by. If it seems that the sound turned into clearly the wind, our brain has misinterpreted the sensory enter based on its expectations. Similarly, in conditions of uncertainty, which includes whilst we are offered with ambiguous visible records, the brain might "fill inside the gaps" primarily based on beyond experiences or contextual cues, leading to a distorted or illusionary belief.

The phenomenon of perceptual filling-in similarly illustrates this predictive manner. When we observe a scene, we would awareness on one component of the surroundings, consisting of a person's face or a particular item. However, the mind fills within the lacking details of the encircling area based totally on previous information and expectations, that can now and again lead to inaccuracies in our notion of the overall scene.

Although our sensory structures are remarkably accurate in lots of conditions, they're not infallible. The presence of sensory illusions indicates that our perceptions of the sector aren't constantly direct reflections of objective fact. Instead, they're shaped by the mind's processing mechanisms, which prioritize performance, survival, and the era of that means.

Fevzi H.

Sensory illusions remind us that what we understand as actual may be a distorted or incomplete representation of the arena.

Moreover, sensory accuracy isn't always uniform across individuals. People with different sensory sensitivities, neurological conditions, or cognitive capabilities may experience illusions differently. For example, a few individuals with synesthesia may also understand sounds as colorations or partner tastes with particular shapes, leading to particular and private experiences of reality. These versions in sensory processing spotlight the subjective nature of belief and the mind's function in constructing individual stories of the arena.

Sensory illusions offer a fascinating glimpse into how the brain constructs our belief of fact. They monitor that our senses do no longer simply passively acquire records however actively interpret and system it, frequently in ways that result in distorted or incomplete representations of the external international. The brain's reliance on prediction, context, and earlier expertise plays a significant function in shaping our revel in of the sector, and when those approaches go awry, sensory illusions arise.

While our sensory systems are fantastically efficient at assisting us navigate the arena, they're now not perfect. The illusions they produce spotlight the complicated and dynamic nature of perception, as well as the ways wherein the brain actively constructs the truth we revel in. Understanding the mechanisms at the back of sensory illusions gives precious insights into the character of perception and the bounds of our capability to perceive objective fact. Ultimately, our sensory reviews remind us that the brain isn't always absolutely a passive receiver of outside stimuli, but an lively player within the creation of the fact we experience.

1.4 Dreams, Hallucinations, and Alternative Realities

The nature of reality, as we perceive it thru our senses, is not restrained to the waking global alone. Our minds are capable of generating entire worlds of enjoy, even inside the absence of external stimuli. These exchange states of recognition—whether or not through dreams, hallucinations, or other styles of altered fact—monitor profound insights into how the mind constructs and translates the sector round us.

Dreams are one of the most enigmatic factors of human attention. Despite centuries of cultural and mental exploration, scientists still have best a partial know-how of why we dream and how these reports emerge. Dreams arise for the duration of the speedy eye movement (REM) level of sleep, a section characterised by using heightened mind interest, rapid eye actions, and vibrant visible and sensory reports.

During REM sleep, the brain is rather lively, often processing feelings, reminiscences, and unresolved conflicts.

Some theories recommend that dreams may additionally serve as a shape of cognitive processing, helping the brain to consolidate recollections, make sense of emotional reviews, or hassle-solve unresolved issues from waking existence. Another theory posits that desires are truely the brain's manner of sorting thru random neural pastime, which is then given that means via the brain's interpretive structures.

Dreams are frequently exceedingly subjective, with imagery, subject matters, and narratives that may be influenced by private reports, fears, goals, and subconscious thoughts. However, a few goals, which includes routine goals, lucid goals, and nightmares, suggest deeper psychological or physiological connections to our waking lives. For instance, lucid dreaming happens while the dreamer turns into privy to the truth that they're dreaming and can actually have the capability to manipulate the occasions in the dream. This type of dream demanding situations our know-how of consciousness and the bounds among the waking global and the dream world.

The content material of dreams can range from mundane stories to surreal or fantastical situations. People frequently report feeling extreme emotions in dreams, from joy to terror, despite the fact that they understand the reports are not actual. These emotional responses highlight the mind's capability to create a vivid and immersive enjoy, despite the reality that the events themselves aren't occurring within the bodily world. Dreams can be deeply symbolic, with specific photos or topics carrying particular meanings associated with the dreamer's psyche. For instance, goals of flying, falling, or being chased are not unusual themes that many humans revel in, regularly reflecting unconscious fears or dreams.

While goals arise in the course of sleep, hallucinations are perceptual studies that get up inside the waking nation, regularly inside the absence of outside stimuli. Hallucinations can have an effect on any of the five senses, from seeing things that are not there (visible hallucinations) to hearing non-existent sounds (auditory hallucinations). Unlike goals, which are typically understood as a shape of inner intellectual processing, hallucinations represent a disruption inside the regular functioning of sensory processing.

Hallucinations can be resulting from a extensive variety of things, from mental situations like schizophrenia to neurological disorders, drug use, sensory deprivation, and even sleep deprivation. For instance, humans with schizophrenia may additionally revel in auditory hallucinations, listening to voices that others do no longer listen, which may be distressing and puzzling. Similarly, people stricken by delirium or mind harm might also enjoy visible hallucinations, along with seeing items or people that aren't present.

In some cases, hallucinations may be triggered deliberately, inclusive of through the use of sure psychedelic substances. These tablets, consisting of LSD, psilocybin (magic mushrooms), and DMT, can adjust the brain's regular sensory processing pathways, leading to profound distortions in belief. People below the affect of these materials can also experience bright and often surreal visions, together with seeing geometric styles, encountering mythical creatures, or experiencing a feel of merging with the universe.

The mechanisms behind hallucinations are complex, concerning adjustments in mind chemistry and neural circuits. Some researchers trust that hallucinations get up from the mind's tendency to generate expectancies based totally on past experiences after which "fill in" sensory gaps whilst external stimuli are inadequate. In the case of visual hallucinations, the mind would possibly generate photos or situations based totally on earlier experiences or emotional states, even supposing no actual visible enter is present. This phenomenon suggests that perception is not a passive procedure but an active construction of the mind, in which the brain is based on internal processes to make feel of the arena.

The experiences of desires and hallucinations assignment the belief of a novel, goal truth. Both of these altered states of recognition advocate that truth is not definitely what's perceived by using the senses, but instead a complex and dynamic assemble created by means of the mind. In the case of desires, the brain constructs entire worlds primarily based on reminiscence, feelings, and imagination, at the same time as in hallucinations, the brain creates sensory studies inside the absence of external stimuli.

This increases the query: if the brain is capable of generating entire worlds of belief without any outside input, what does that say approximately the nature of fact itself? If the mind can create bright reports of the sector primarily based totally on internal procedures, is our perception of the external world any more "real" than the worlds we enjoy in desires or hallucinations?

Philosophers have lengthy debated the nature of fact and belief. Some have argued that every one of our stories are subjective and that we are able to in no way simply know the objective world beyond our senses. The idea that reality is built via the mind, in place of without a doubt acquired passively, suggests that our perceptions may be more flexible and malleable than we realise. In this sense, dreams and hallucinations aren't simply anomalies or deviations from ordinary notion; they're integral to the human revel in and offer treasured insights into the mind's ability to construct alternative realities.

One fascinating factor of each dreams and hallucinations is their ability to blur the limits among what's "real" and what's "imagined." In each cases, the experiences are noticeably shiny and immersive, frequently leaving individuals thinking whether or not they're certainly experiencing reality or something else completely. For example, individuals who revel in lucid desires are acutely conscious that they are dreaming, however within the dream, they'll feel as though they're in a very actual and tangible world. Similarly, people who experience hallucinations may additionally interact with hallucinated gadgets or human beings as although they're actual, even though they don't have any bodily lifestyles.

This blurring of obstacles has implications for our expertise of cognizance and the mind. If the brain is able to creating studies that feel as actual as the ones encountered in the physical world, it challenges the belief that perception is an immediate reflection of objective reality. Instead, it indicates that reality is, in element, a product of the thoughts's internal strategies, influenced by means of recollections, emotions, and expectations. This view aligns with theories in philosophy and neuroscience that advocate truth is not a fixed and goal element, however a constantly changing and subjective experience formed through the brain.

Dreams, hallucinations, and alternative realities monitor the fluidity of human perception and task our information of what is real. Both desires and hallucinations exhibit that the mind is not a passive receiver of sensory information, however an energetic player in constructing the sector we revel in. While desires arise during sleep, creating bright and regularly symbolic situations, hallucinations stand up within the waking kingdom, disrupting ordinary sensory processing and leading to distorted or totally fabricated reviews.

These altered states of consciousness enhance profound questions about the nature of reality and belief. If the mind is able to growing entire worlds of revel in, what does that say approximately our perception of the outside international? Are our waking reviews any greater "actual" than the ones we encounter in goals or hallucinations? Ultimately, the look at of desires, hallucinations, and opportunity realities gives precious insights into the brain's complicated strategies of perception and highlights the malleability of human focus.

1.5 The Neuroscience of Perception: How Reality Is Coded in Our Brain

Perception is the process via which we interpret and make feel of the world round us, shaping our knowledge of reality. It isn't a mere mirrored image of the outside global but a complicated cognitive method that is constructed with the aid of the brain. Our senses gather statistics from the surroundings, however it is the mind that organizes and interprets this information, creating our subjective enjoy of fact.

The human mind is prepared with exceptionally specialised structures that allow it to perceive, manner, and interpret sensory statistics. Our sensory organs—eyes, ears, skin, nose, and tongue—are the primary line of verbal exchange with the world. They acquire stimuli from the environment and convert them into electrical signals which can be transmitted to the brain. However, the brain does not passively get hold of these indicators; as an alternative, it actively interprets and constructs our perception of truth.

At the heart of perception is the mind's potential to make sense of incoming sensory records with the aid of integrating statistics from special senses and comparing it with existing information. This method isn't always always a sincere reflection of the outside global; the mind is constantly making predictions and changes based totally on beyond experiences and contextual factors. In essence, belief is a optimistic process, where the mind fills in gaps in sensory statistics and adjusts its expertise to make sense of ambiguous or incomplete information.

The mind's perceptual structures rely closely on neural networks and circuits that involve more than one areas of the mind. For example, the number one visible cortex approaches visible facts, even as the auditory cortex approaches sound. However, better-order regions of the mind, such as the prefrontal cortex, are responsible for integrating this sensory information with memory, interest, and cognitive capabilities. It is right here that our subjective enjoy of truth begins to take form, because the mind translates sensory enter in the context of our feelings, past studies, and expectations.

The mind's processing of sensory records begins the moment it receives alerts from the sensory organs. This technique occurs in levels, with each level adding layers of complexity to the information being processed. For example, whilst we see an object, light enters the eye and is centered onto the retina, where it's far converted into electric indicators by photoreceptor cells. These signals are then despatched to the visible cortex in the back of the brain, where they are similarly processed to identify shapes, colorations, and movement.

But vision isn't always just about detecting mild and shade; it entails better-degree processing that facilitates us recognize what we are seeing. The mind takes into consideration context, earlier knowledge, and even expectations approximately what we must be seeing. This is why our notion of the arena is often influenced by way of what we already realize or assume to encounter. For instance, if we're in a familiar setting, the brain uses that context to make predictions about what items are possibly to be present and how they need to look, which can every now and then result in misperceptions or illusions while matters deviate from what is predicted.

Similarly, the auditory gadget works by using detecting sound waves that enter the ear, which can be then transformed

Fevzi H.

into electrical indicators that the mind strategies. The auditory cortex translates those alerts, permitting us to understand sounds and make experience of speech. The brain also integrates auditory information with visual and tactile information, helping us recognize the context of the sounds we listen. For example, when we hear someone speakme, our mind now not best methods the sound of the phrases however also interprets the emotional tone and context of the verbal exchange based on visible cues, like facial expressions and frame language.

The integration of sensory statistics is a essential element of belief. The mind constantly combines input from one of a kind senses, which includes sight, hearing, and contact, to create a unified and coherent notion of the arena. This multisensory integration allows us to navigate our environment efficiently, from spotting faces to deciphering the placement of items in area. However, this integration can also lead to sensory conflicts that have an impact on our belief, including whilst visual and auditory records do now not suit, main to reviews like the McGurk effect, wherein we perceive a unique sound based on what we see.

While sensory processing is the muse of notion, it's miles the brain's attention mechanisms and cognitive features that form and refine our enjoy. Attention performs a central role in figuring out which sensory records is prioritized and processed

Mind and Simulation

in element, and which statistics is unnoticed. This selective attention lets in us to cognizance on essential stimuli in our environment at the same time as filtering out irrelevant or distracting facts.

Attention is a dynamic and flexible technique, permitting us to shift consciousness based on the demands of the scenario. For instance, when we are using, our interest is typically focused on the road and the surrounding traffic, filtering out different less applicable sensory input, like the communique happening inside the vehicle. This capacity to selectively attend to positive stimuli is governed through the mind's attentional networks, which include regions together with the parietal cortex and the frontal lobe.

However, interest is not always perfectly correct. The brain's cognitive biases, prompted by emotions, past studies, and expectancies, can distort belief. For example, a person who has a fear of puppies may be hypervigilant to any sign of a canine in their surroundings, even mistaking a shadow or form for a real canine. This attentional bias ends in a heightened belief of risk, even if there is no on the spot hazard. In this manner, our feelings and cognitive techniques can form the way we understand the world, on occasion main to distortions or misinterpretations.

Additionally, top-down processing, wherein the mind applies prior expertise and expectations to interpret sensory input, also can influence notion. When we're supplied with ambiguous or incomplete statistics, the brain uses context and enjoy to fill inside the gaps and make sense of what we are seeing or hearing. For example, whilst reading a sentence with missing letters or phrases, we're regularly able to fill in the blanks based on our information of language and context, permitting us to understand the meaning in spite of the unfinished statistics. However, this reliance on earlier knowledge also can cause illusions or misperceptions, including seeing faces in inanimate objects or hearing voices in random noise.

Despite the mind's remarkable capability to assemble an accurate illustration of the arena, it's far susceptible to errors. Perceptual illusions occur whilst the brain misinterprets sensory information, creating a distorted or incorrect notion of fact. These illusions display the complexities of the way the brain tactics sensory enter and the numerous factors that have an effect on belief.

Visual illusions, consisting of the Müller-Lyer phantasm (where two lines of same length seem like specific), spotlight how the brain makes use of contextual cues to interpret length and distance. In this situation, the brain is predicated on prior information approximately how lines generally behave inside the world, main it to understand one line as being longer than the opposite, even though they are the same duration. Similarly, auditory illusions, such as the Shepard tone (which creates the illusion of a constantly ascending pitch), reveal how the brain approaches sound in a manner that may lead to perceptual errors.

Perceptual illusions aren't just curiosities; they provide precious insights into the mind's underlying mechanisms of notion. By analyzing those illusions, neuroscientists can analyze greater about how the mind processes sensory records, makes predictions, and constructs our subjective revel in of fact. Illusions monitor the complex interplay among sensory input, interest, memory, and cognitive procedures, highlighting how the mind's interpretation of the world is not continually a devoted representation of objective reality.

One of the maximum charming components of perception is its plasticity—the mind's ability to adapt and alternate its perceptual tactics primarily based on experience. This neural plasticity lets in us to research and adapt to new environments, as well as recover from injuries that have an effect on sensory processing. For example, whilst a person loses their sight, the brain compensates via improving the closing senses, including contact and listening to, to assist navigate the environment.

Similarly, the brain's perceptual systems are continuously fashioned by using enjoy. People who have interaction in sports that require heightened sensory recognition, which include musicians or athletes, may expand specialized perceptual abilities that permit them to manner facts extra successfully or with more precision. This adaptability suggests that notion is not a hard and fast or rigid technique, however a dynamic and bendy one this is formed by the mind's ongoing interaction with the sector.

Perception is not honestly a passive system of receiving sensory data; it's miles an lively and dynamic creation of fact that includes complicated interactions among sensory enter, attention, memory, and cognition. The mind continuously integrates data from distinct sensory structures, makes predictions based on beyond studies, and adapts its processes based on contextual factors and attentional demands. However, this procedure is not infallible, and the brain is vulnerable to mistakes in notion, leading to illusions and misinterpretations of the world.

The neuroscience of belief provides precious insights into how the brain constructs our revel in of truth and the way it shapes our information of the arena. While the mind's capability to generate a coherent and immersive enjoy of fact is excellent, it also highlights the limitations of our belief and the malleability of human attention. By analyzing how the brain methods sensory statistics, we are able to benefit a deeper knowledge of the mind's role in shaping our experience of the arena and the methods in which reality is encoded in our brains.

Fevzi H.

CHAPTER 2

Philosophical Perspectives on Simulation Theory

2.1 Plato's Allegory of the Cave: Is the World We See Just a Shadow?

Plato's Allegory of the Cave stands as one of the cornerstones of Western philosophy, supporting us understand the difference among fact and perception. The allegory highlights how the concept of "truth" is constructed in another way for every individual and the way our manner of perceiving the world is probably significantly confined. Plato's comparison among the world of paperwork and the shadows at the cave wall serves as a profound metaphor that aligns with modern interpretations of simulation concept.

In Plato's Allegory of the Cave, humans are depicted as prisoners trapped in a dark cave, watching shadows projected onto a wall. These prisoners had been chained in the sort of way that they are able to simplest see the shadows of items behind them. These shadows are mere reflections of the actual global outdoor the cave. The prisoners, having by no means seen the outside world, take delivery of those shadows as truth. One of the prisoners ultimately escapes and sees the light outdoor the cave. At first, the brightness blinds him, however through the years, he turns into acquainted with the genuine world and knows the character of fact. He returns to the cave to tell the others, however they resist his claims and reject the concept that there is some thing past their shadows.

This allegory serves as a deep metaphor for cutting-edge-day simulation theories, thinking whether or not the sector we understand is certainly actual or merely a illustration. Much just like the prisoners inside the cave, we may be limited to a restricted information of fact, where what we enjoy is handiest a "shadow" of the actual world. The idea that the sector we revel in is not the actual truth is a perception that aligns with the hypothesis of simulation theory, wherein our perceptions are just a simulated version of a far larger and extra complicated fact.

In Plato's philosophy, the real nature of fact lies in the realm of the "Forms," that are abstract, perfect, and eternal ideals. The bodily international, in step with Plato, is simply an imperfect illustration of these ideals. This perception parallels simulation idea's important question: Is the world we understand simply actual, or is it only a simulation? In simulation principle, the universe is proposed to be an artificial assemble—created perhaps by an advanced intelligence, like a supercomputer or AI. Similarly, Plato's Forms advocate that what we experience through our senses is an insignificant mirrored image of a higher, more best truth.

Both Plato's principle and simulation principle recommend that our understanding of reality is inherently restricted and that the real nature of life is past what we are able to perceive or believe. If we comply with Plato's reasoning, the world we experience might be analogous to the shadows on the cave wall—handiest a faint glimpse of some thing far extra complex and profound. The notion that fact could be an artificial simulation does no longer appear a long way-fetched when considered via the lens of Plato's idealism.

Simulation principle aligns intently with the perception that, just like Plato's prisoners, we can be restrained to an synthetic reality with constrained get right of entry to to what in reality exists. If the arena is indeed a simulation, then we, as its population, are not any one of a kind from the prisoners within the cave, most effective able to see and apprehend what is presented to us within the parameters of the simulation. In the case of virtual worlds, augmented realities, and virtual simulations, we may additionally emerge as extra disconnected from the bodily world and start to simply accept those built experiences because the best authentic shape of fact.

Yet, just because the prisoner who escapes the cave realizes the truth approximately the arena, people who are aware about the idea of simulation concept can also searching for to recognize the proper nature of existence, beyond what is given to them. This concept challenges the manner we interpret our sensory studies. In present day times, virtual reality has delivered a brand new layer of simulation in our lives, in which digital worlds mimic the physical global, however they nonetheless best constitute a restrained model of reality. The query remains: if our perceptions are ruled through a better assemble, are we able to ever damage unfastened and experience the "out of doors international"?

Simulation concept, while mixed with Plato's philosophy, offers a deeper examination of ways focus pertains to the concept of truth. If our sensory stories and perceptions are based on a simulation, how are we able to declare to recognise whatever approximately the actual nature of the sector? Plato's view suggests that human knowledge is confined to the area of appearances, but deeper awareness lies inside the intellectual and best realm. In the same vein, simulation theory argues that our aware reviews might be mere projections created with the aid of a higher system.

In this context, cognizance itself won't be an natural function of the mind, but alternatively an emergent belongings of the simulation. This increases an excellent greater profound query: if we live in a simulation, is our recognition an artifact of the simulated surroundings, or is there a way for our minds to go beyond the limits of this device and understand the underlying reality? Plato's metaphor of the prisoners in the cave suggests that breaking free from the simulation requires a shift in belief—a motion from ignorance to know-how, from shadow to mild.

Plato's Allegory of the Cave, while viewed via the lens of simulation principle, activates us to invite: what's truth? If our

Fevzi H.

notion of the sector is restrained and primarily based on a simulation, how are we able to ever really recognize the nature of life? Simulation principle and Plato's idealism both point to the possibility that our sensory perceptions are simply shadows of a more profound fact. This realization challenges the very essence of human recognition and forces us to reconsider the boundaries of what's real and what's phantasm.

The allegory and simulation concept in the long run propose that if our life is indeed a simulation, then our information of the arena is inherently unsuitable. Just as the prisoners inside the cave are unable to realize the sector beyond the shadows, so too might also we be confined within a simulation that restricts our information of actual truth. In this example, the pursuit of know-how and wisdom will become no longer just an intellectual exercising, but a look for the underlying code that can monitor the actual nature of lifestyles. Just because the prisoners should get away the cave to peer the light, we too ought to strive to interrupt loose from the simulation to glimpse the real global beyond.

2.2 Descartes and the Doubtful Nature of Reality: I Think, Therefore I Am?

René Descartes, frequently appeared as the daddy of modern philosophy, famously proposed the concept "Cogito, ergo sum" ("I assume, therefore I am") as a foundational reality in know-how lifestyles. This announcement turned into a reaction to his radical skepticism—his approach of doubting the whole lot, inclusive of the very life of the outside global and his very own body. Descartes' method, called Cartesian skepticism, aligns strikingly with the modern-day questions surrounding simulation theory and the character of reality. Descartes' meditations offer a profound exploration of doubt, cognizance, and the bounds of human expertise, which are critical to the continuing debate approximately whether or not our fact is proper or simply a simulation.

Descartes' philosophical adventure began with what he called methodical doubt, a process via which he doubted the whole lot he knew to be true to be able to arrive at some thing indubitable. In his work Meditations on First Philosophy, Descartes puzzled the very existence of the external world, together with the physical frame, the universe, or even his own mind. He reasoned that it became viable that every one of those can be illusions created via an external pressure or a deceiving demon—an idea that parallels the idea of a simulated fact in which a complicated entity would possibly manipulate the belief of an individual.

Descartes' skepticism even extended to the reliability of his senses, which will be deceived, as within the case of optical illusions or goals. He postulated that our senses won't reflect an external, goal fact at all. This doubt of the senses mirrors

Fevzi H.

present day simulation theory, which shows that the sensory experiences we perceive is probably artificially generated, main us to impeach if we are able to ever actually accept as true with what we experience.

The question of "What is real?" turns into not only a philosophical inquiry but a critical consideration in the context of simulation theory. If the nature of reality can be doubted on this manner, what ensures will we have that the arena round us isn't always clearly a simulation designed to deceive us? Descartes' argument, though developed centuries earlier than the idea of digital fact or virtual simulations, affords the highbrow foundation for knowledge how we might exist within a simulated universe, and the way our perceptions might be distorted by using an unseen pressure.

While Descartes doubted the whole thing, he ultimately arrived at the belief that the very act of doubting required a thinking challenge to carry out the act of doubt. Hence, his well-known end, Cogito, ergo sum—"I think, therefore I am"—became the only undeniable truth. Descartes argued that the life of his personal thoughts or focus could not be doubted due to the fact although a malicious demon had been deceiving him approximately the outside international, the very act of being deceived required a questioning, aware entity to be deceived.

This philosophical perception serves as a important anchor within the look for truth amidst uncertainty. For Descartes, the mind—our ability to think, doubt, and purpose—changed into the inspiration of life. In the context of simulation concept, this raises an crucial question: If we're indeed dwelling in a simulation, what's the nature of the mind inside that simulation? Descartes' emphasis at the thinking difficulty highlights that even inside a simulated reality, the thoughts might nevertheless exist independently of the simulated international, keeping its capacity for doubt, reasoning, and self-recognition. However, if the entire universe is a simulation, then what does it suggest for the character of consciousness? Can focus sincerely exist with out a physical reality to interact with?

Descartes introduced the idea of the evil demon—an all-effective being that could potentially misinform us into believing that the outside world exists as we perceive it, when in reality, it is probably absolutely fabricated. This concept foreshadows modern simulation idea, wherein the "evil demon" is replaced with the concept of a superintelligent entity or advanced artificial intelligence that creates and controls a simulated truth. In this situation, our perceptions of the sector aren't a reflection of an objective, outside fact but are instead manipulated via an outside force, much like how a simulated surroundings could be managed through a computer.

The similarities among Descartes' evil demon and simulation idea are hanging. In each instances, the thoughts is trapped in a built fact, unable to verify the authentic nature of lifestyles. Just as Descartes puzzled whether we will accept as true with our senses, simulation idea challenges us to question whether or not we will consider any of our perceptions if they are being created via a simulation. Is our expertise of reality clearly a fabrication, much like Descartes' imagined global of deception?

Descartes' emphasis at the thoughts as the foundation of reality in a world complete of doubt resonates deeply with current worries about the character of consciousness within the realm of simulation theory. If we are dwelling in a simulated global, then the mind's interaction with that simulation will become a key factor of attention. Descartes maintained that the mind is separate from the body, a idea called dualism. This view raises intriguing questions about the character of the mind in a simulated reality: if the mind can think independently of the frame in the bodily international, ought to it additionally feature in a simulation? Would the mind nonetheless have business enterprise in a international where each sensory revel in is managed and crafted by using an external force?

Furthermore, Descartes believed that expertise of the outside global is mediated via the senses, but the senses can be deceived. In the case of simulation idea, the thoughts could still perceive a constructed truth, probably manipulated by a higher intelligence. This raises the query of whether our recognition is able to breaking unfastened from the simulated confines to acquire actual information or if it's miles permanently restrained to experiencing a fabricated reality.

Descartes' skepticism and subsequent declaration that the thoughts is the most effective indubitable foundation for understanding continue to be a important point in philosophical debates approximately the nature of fact. Yet simulation theory expands upon Descartes' authentic skepticism, suggesting that no longer most effective can our senses lie to us, but the entire international we experience is probably an illusion, controlled by way of an external, artificial machine. This view broadens the scope of Descartes' original doubt by way of implying that the outside world itself might not exist within the manner we understand it.

If simulation theory holds, and our truth is artificially built, Descartes' declare that the thoughts is the muse of reality could be similarly examined. In a simulated global, the thoughts is probably an critical detail, however its reviews could be constrained by means of the structure of the simulation. Does Descartes' dualism—his separation of mind and body—nonetheless practice if the bodily global is an illusion? Or is the thoughts itself merely a element of the simulation, existing in the parameters set through the artificial machine?

Fevzi H.

René Descartes' philosophical exploration of doubt and the nature of fact offers a profound basis for cutting-edge discussions approximately the character of existence, especially in relation to simulation theory. Descartes' Cogito, ergo sum underscores the central role of attention in know-how fact, but simulation theory complicates this via thinking the reality of the arena in which cognizance exists. Whether in a international of outside deception or in a simulated universe, Descartes' skepticism stays a pivotal tool for know-how the bounds of human information and the position of notion in shaping our reports.

As we keep to discover the philosophical implications of simulation principle, Descartes' paintings serves as a touchstone for comparing how our minds system, interpret, and ultimately query the fact wherein we exist. In a international that is probably a simulation, the core query stays: if we are deceived, how are we able to ever honestly recognize what's real?

2.3 Berkeley and Idealism: If Matter Doesn't Exist, What is Reality?

The idea of idealism, as proposed by way of the 18th-century logician George Berkeley, gives a charming lens thru which to view the character of fact—one that resonates deeply with modern discussions approximately simulation concept.

Berkeley's idealism challenges the not unusual assumption that the bodily world exists independently of our perception of it. His famous dictum, "esse est percipi" (to be is to be perceived), asserts that truth consists only of minds and their ideas. In other words, the external global does now not exist outdoor of the perceptions of conscious beings, and fabric gadgets are best actual insofar as they're perceived.

Berkeley's idealism, at the beginning look, seems notably one of a kind from the materialist worldview, where the bodily universe exists independently of human perception. Yet, when taken into consideration inside the context of simulation theory, Berkeley's thoughts appear to have a surprising relevance to modern philosophical questions about the nature of fact.

George Berkeley's idealism stems from his radical task to the materialist thought of truth. According to Berkeley, the life of objects is entirely dependent on their being perceived. Without a thoughts to perceive them, gadgets quit to exist. In his work A Treatise Concerning the Principles of Human Knowledge, Berkeley argues that all bodily gadgets are actually ideas in the thoughts, and these ideas are sustained via God, who constantly perceives and sustains the world in existence. For Berkeley, there's no need for a cloth substance to explain the arena round us. Rather, the whole thing we enjoy—whether or not it be a rock, a tree, or a planet—is in reality an idea inside the thoughts, an item of notion.

This view fundamentally challenges the materialist assumption that objects exist independently of the mind. Berkeley's argument hinges on the concept that our sensory reports—sight, contact, taste, and so on—are not the result of interactions with a mind-independent global however are rather a part of a mental framework. The outside international, in Berkeley's view, isn't made of fabric materials, however is as an alternative a collection of perceptions, which can be sustained with the aid of a divine mind. The question of ways truth can exist with out material gadgets is responded through Berkeley with the announcement that all things exist within the thoughts of God.

The connection between Berkeley's idealism and simulation idea becomes obvious while we recall the character of perception in a simulated reality. If our perceptions of the world are the result of a simulation, then, just like Berkeley's idealism, the outside world may not exist independently of our belief of it. In a simulated universe, the whole thing that we revel in—every object, every landscape, every person—exists because the simulation is designed to supply those stories for us. The international does now not exist outdoor of the simulation; it exists due to the fact it is being perceived by way of us, the population of the simulation.

Simulation concept, which posits that our reality is a pc-generated simulation, has many parallels to Berkeley's idealism. In a simulation, the "bodily" world around us will be nothing greater than an illusion created with the aid of a sophisticated computer machine. Just as Berkeley's idealism denies the existence of an external, cloth global, simulation principle suggests that the physical universe we perceive isn't "real" within the conventional feel, but is rather a chain of perceptions generated via a computational machine.

In both Berkeley's philosophy and simulation idea, perception performs a vital position in constituting fact. Berkeley's idealism asserts that items exist best insofar as they're perceived, and simulation theory argues that our sensory reviews aren't interactions with an outside global, but interactions with a simulated surroundings. Both perspectives advise that truth isn't always an unbiased entity but is alternatively deeply intertwined with the perceptions of aware beings.

For Berkeley, the life of gadgets relies upon at the belief of these objects. If we stop perceiving an item, it ceases to exist. In a simulation, this idea finds a striking echo: if we have been to by hook or by crook disconnect from the simulation or prevent perceiving the simulated world, the gadgets inside it'd give up to exist as properly. The entire universe in a simulation is not anything greater than a chain of facts points and sensory

Fevzi H.

inputs, created and maintained by the computational device. In this way, Berkeley's idealism and simulation concept both undermine the perception of a thoughts-independent fabric world.

Berkeley's idealism ends in an interesting query: what is the function of the mind in developing fact? For Berkeley, the mind—in particular the mind of God—is the last perceiver that sustains the life of the sector. However, inside the context of simulation idea, the position of the mind is transferred to the creators of the simulation. In this example, the conscious thoughts (whether or not human or artificial) is experiencing a truth that is designed, generated, and managed by an external source.

This raises interesting questions on the character of awareness and its dating to reality. In Berkeley's idealism, attention is the source of all truth, as the arena exists best as it's miles perceived by minds. In a simulation, cognizance—whether or not human or synthetic—perceives the sector within the confines of the simulation, however that perception is generated by way of an outside computational device. The thoughts is still crucial to the development of truth, however its perceptions are mediated through the simulation, tons as Berkeley's mind is based at the divine to keep the fact of the sector.

Mind and Simulation

One of Berkeley's key contributions to philosophy was his task to the notion of cloth substance. According to Berkeley, cloth substances—matters that exist independently of the thoughts—do not exist. All that exists are thoughts within the thoughts, and these thoughts are sustained via God. In a similar vein, simulation concept indicates that the bodily international, as we perceive it, is an phantasm. The gadgets we see, contact, and engage with may not exist in a material sense but are alternatively the made from a simulation designed to create the illusion of a cloth world.

If the arena is a simulation, then, similar to Berkeley's thoughts, the gadgets we understand aren't "actual" within the traditional experience. The chair you are sitting in, the ground beneath your ft, and the sky above you're all part of the simulated surroundings that you enjoy. These objects might not have unbiased existence, but they are real insofar as they may be a part of the simulated fact created so as to perceive. This reflects Berkeley's view that the bodily global is nothing greater than a collection of perceptions sustained through a thoughts.

In Berkeley's idealism, the world is in the end sustained by using the mind of God, who guarantees that the sector continues to exist even when people are not perceiving it. In simulation concept, the world is sustained via the computational energy of the simulation's creators, who're chargeable for retaining the arena and ensuring that it maintains to feature as a coherent, interactive gadget. Just as Berkeley believed that God become the closing perceiver and sustainer of the arena, simulation theory indicates that there may be a writer or set of creators who maintain the simulation in which we exist.

This parallel between Berkeley's idealism and simulation idea increases intriguing philosophical questions on the nature of the thoughts, the function of belief in developing fact, and the capacity for a author or controlling force at the back of our truth. Whether we're residing in a international sustained by way of divine notion or in a global sustained with the aid of advanced technology, the query remains: if rely doesn't exist independently of perception, what, then, is the nature of fact?

George Berkeley's idealism offers a notion-frightening perspective on the nature of reality, one that demanding situations the conventional materialist view and resonates strongly with the questions posed by simulation concept. Both idealism and simulation idea recommend that the sector we perceive may not be an objective, mind-unbiased truth but is as an alternative a assemble of perception, either in the thoughts or within a simulated system. The query of what constitutes reality isn't without difficulty spoke back, however Berkeley's ideas assist illuminate the profound philosophical implications of the simulation speculation. If depend does not exist in the manner we historically understand it, then truth itself may be some distance extra elusive, complicated, and depending on perception than we ever imagined.

2.4 Bostrom's Simulation Argument: What is Real in the Universe?

In the twenty first century, one of the most influential contributions to the discussion of simulation concept came from logician Nick Bostrom. In 2003, Bostrom provided the now-well-known Simulation Argument, which suggests that it is viable—or even in all likelihood—that our entire reality is a computer-generated simulation created by using a greater advanced civilization. Bostrom's argument has emerge as a relevant factor of dialogue in each philosophy and technological know-how fiction, with many brooding about whether we're living in a simulation or whether or not our perceptions of the universe replicate a actual, "actual" world.

Bostrom's simulation argument is based on a chain of probabilistic claims, grounded within the idea that at the least one in all 3 propositions should be actual:

1. The Human Species Will Go Extinct Before Reaching a Posthuman Stage: This proposition shows that humanity will in no way broaden the technological abilties to create sensible, large-scale simulations of cognizance. There can be a technological barrier or existential risk that prevents us from

Fevzi H.

attaining this advanced kingdom, which means that simulated realities could in no way come to exist.

2. A Posthuman Civilization Would Be Unlikely to Simulate Realistic Consciousnesses: This possibility posits that although humanity does reach a posthuman kingdom with the ability to simulate attention, it might select now not to create these simulations. The motivations for no longer doing so will be moral, philosophical, or associated with the dangers of creating sizeable, aware entities within simulations.

3. We Are Almost Certainly Living in a Simulation: The 0.33 proposition is the maximum controversial and the only that has generated the most debate. According to Bostrom, if the primary two propositions are fake—which means that advanced civilizations do expand the era to simulate attention and pick to accomplish that—then the number of simulated realities ought to massively outnumber "real" realities. In this case, the chances folks dwelling in a simulation boom dramatically. If there are billions of simulated worlds and simplest a small range of "real" worlds, it's miles statistically more likely that we are residing in a simulated reality.

Bostrom's argument is constructed on the idea that, if a technologically superior civilization has the capability to simulate awareness, it would be capable of growing simulations so realistic that the simulated beings inner them might now not be able to differentiate the simulation from "fact." Given this, the variety of simulations ought to outnumber the actual worlds, and the possibility of residing in a simulation could end up very excessive.

The core of Bostrom's argument lies in statistical reasoning. If future civilizations are capable of create simulations of cognizance, and in the event that they select to accomplish that, the wide variety of simulated aware beings might far surpass the wide variety of actual humans. In a hypothetical destiny with a virtually endless range of simulations, the range of simulated realities could weigh down the number of actual, physical realities.

To illustrate this idea, Bostrom uses a probabilistic technique: if we are living in a world in which posthuman civilizations have the potential to simulate conscious beings, then the sheer quantity of simulated entities would make it overwhelmingly probable that we're one among them. The argument rests on the belief that, given sufficient time, a posthuman civilization could be exceedingly inspired to create severa simulations, perhaps for clinical, ancient, or leisure functions. The more simulations there are, the more statistically in all likelihood it becomes that we're dwelling in a single.

This concept experiment introduces an exciting paradox: if we're dwelling in a simulation, what's the nature of "reality" that we trust to be actual? Our experiences, interactions, and perceptions would be simply as real to us as the reports of someone in a "real" international. Yet, from a cosmic attitude, we can be no greater real than the characters in a pc recreation.

Bostrom's simulation argument raises profound questions about the character of truth itself. If we take delivery of that we could be living in a simulation, it challenges our expertise of lifestyles. What does it imply to be "real" in a universe that may not be "real" within the manner we historically understand it? Is fact the result of a bodily, unbiased international, or is it a assemble designed by means of a greater superior intelligence?

These questions result in a reevaluation of our primary assumptions approximately life. If we are in a simulation, then our perception of the bodily global—the solar, the celebs, the Earth—may want to all be fabricated, designed to create a coherent narrative for the inhabitants of the simulation. The seemingly solid gadgets, the laws of physics, and the passage of time may be no greater than illusions created by a computational gadget. In this scenario, the "real" international may additionally lie beyond the simulation, but it's miles not possible to without delay get right of entry to or recognize it.

In this mild, the query of whether we stay in a simulation turns into now not only a philosophical curiosity, however a profound assignment to our theory of truth. It forces us to reconsider what constitutes "the real international" and whether or not some thing may be said to be absolutely real if it exists totally inside a simulation.

Bostrom's argument also delves into the technological and moral issues surrounding the creation of simulations. If advanced civilizations have the ability to simulate cognizance, must they? What ethical responsibilities could such civilizations have toward the simulated beings they invent? These questions aren't simply theoretical; they invite us to mirror on the ethical implications of creating simulations of conscious beings and the ability outcomes for each the creators and the created.

If simulations are created with conscious entities that revel in ache, joy, or struggling, then the ethical quandary turns into urgent: should the creators of those simulations be responsible for the nicely-being of their simulated inhabitants? Should the simulated entities have rights, or is their life simply a means to an give up for the creators of the simulation? These moral issues convey into cognizance the capacity ethical implications of superior technology, specially in terms of artificial consciousness and the creation of simulated realities.

Bostrom's simulation argument additionally brings to the forefront the philosophical trouble of solipsism—the belief that best one's personal mind and perceptions are certain to exist. If we're residing in a simulation, we can also query the existence of everything outside of our perceived truth. Are the humans around us real, or are they really programs running inside the simulation? Is there a "actual" world past the simulation, and in that case, how are we able to ever get admission to it or understand some thing approximately it?

The simulation argument, in this experience, brings solipsism into the world of technological know-how and generation, asking whether or not the world we experience is virtually impartial of our minds, or whether or not it's miles merely a construct within a huge and complex simulation. In many ways, the simulation argument amplifies the solipsistic worries raised by way of Berkeley's idealism, as both perspectives recommend that what we perceive as reality may be far greater tenuous than we ever imagined.

Nick Bostrom's simulation argument has had a profound effect on contemporary philosophical and scientific discussions approximately the nature of reality. It presents a compelling case that, given the ability for advanced civilizations to create simulations, the chance of dwelling in a simulated fact may be much higher than we think. The argument challenges our maximum fundamental assumptions approximately the universe, inviting us to rethink the very nature of life and our vicinity in the cosmos.

By exploring the consequences of Bostrom's argument, we come to a deeper understanding of what it way to be "actual" in a universe that might not be as we perceive it. The simulation argument does not simply mission our perspectives of physics, era, and ethics—it forces us to confront the very nature of fact itself. If we are indeed living in a simulation, then what's actual? And more importantly, what does it imply to be actual within the first location?

2.5 The Historical Evolution of the Concept of Simulation

The concept that reality won't be what it appears and that our perceptions might be inspired or even constructed via an external pressure has a long and fascinating records. The idea of simulation, as we apprehend it these days, has advanced over centuries, formed via philosophical, medical, and technological advancements. The journey from ancient metaphysical musings to modern technological theories of simulated realities well-knownshows a lot about humanity's ongoing quest to understand the character of lifestyles and our area within the universe.

The earliest philosophical musings approximately simulation may be traced again to historic thinkers who puzzled the nature of notion and truth. The concept that the arena we experience might be an illusion or a trifling projection was famously explored by Plato in his Allegory of the Cave (round 380 BCE). In this allegory, Plato describes prisoners chained internal a cave, who can only see shadows solid at the wall through gadgets behind them. These prisoners mistake the shadows for reality because they've by no means visible the gadgets themselves. This allegory highlights the possibility that what we perceive as reality might be just a faint, distorted mirrored image of a deeper reality, a subject matter that could resonate through the centuries as discussions about phantasm and reality spread out.

The concept of illusion and the character of truth were similarly explored by later philosophers, inclusive of Descartes, whose Meditations on First Philosophy (1641) brought the idea of radical doubt. Descartes famously puzzled the veracity of all things, even his own life, considering that he might be under the impact of a deceptive demon—an external pressure controlling his perceptions. While Descartes did not explicitly body this as a "simulation," his philosophical musings would lay the groundwork for later thoughts that would hyperlink deception and the development of fact to technological and metaphysical constructs.

As medical thought stepped forward, so did the exploration of the connection among reality and notion. In the 17th and 18th centuries, the development of empiricism and rationalism caused new approaches of knowledge the senses and the thoughts's role in shaping our experience of the sector. Thinkers like John Locke, George Berkeley, and Immanuel Kant addressed the nature of truth and perception, in the end influencing the discourse that might surround simulation principle.

Berkeley, as an example, famously argued for idealism—the perception that fabric gadgets do no longer exist independently of the thoughts. In his work A Treatise Concerning the Principles of Human Knowledge (1710), he proposed that truth is entirely built by means of perception and that each one lifestyles depends on the mind of God. While Berkeley did not body his thoughts in terms of simulation, his argument that the external global is depending on perception aligns with later notions of fact as a construct, foreshadowing contemporary ideas of simulated or digital realities.

Immanuel Kant, in his Critique of Pure Reason (1781), presented a greater nuanced perspective with the aid of positing that humans can't recognize the world as it absolutely is, simplest as it seems to us through the lens of our sensory schools and mental categories. Kant's work raised questions about the boundaries of human notion, suggesting that we can never get admission to the "thing-in-itself" (the true nature of truth) and that our reports are continually mediated with the aid of the structures of the thoughts. This raises the possibility that our reports, and hence our information of reality, might be inherently limited and potentially manipulated by external forces—a topic relevant to the concept of simulations.

The twentieth century witnessed the rapid advancement of technology, and with it, new discussions approximately the nature of truth started out to take shape. The development of computing, virtual truth, and cybernetics delivered the opportunity that reality will be artificially built or manipulated by means of machines. In the mid-twentieth century, thinkers like Norbert Wiener, who based the sphere of cybernetics, explored the concept of structures of manipulate and remarks loops in each biological and mechanical structures. These thoughts could later impact discussions about synthetic intelligence and simulations, suggesting that machines might sooner or later simulate focus and reality itself.

In the area of technological know-how fiction, the concept of simulated realities have become a distinguished subject matter in the late 20th century. Works like The Matrix (1999) and Neuromancer (1984) delivered the idea of simulated worlds to the forefront of famous way of life. These testimonies depicted characters living in simulated environments that have been indistinguishable from "real" fact, raising questions about the nature of consciousness, freedom, and the manage exerted through powerful entities. The idea that simulations might be so superior that they might be not possible to distinguish from real reality captured the imagination of each the general public and philosophers alike.

The concept of simulation principle as we understand it these days owes a great deal to the work of philosopher Nick Bostrom, who in 2003 formulated the Simulation Argument, which suggests that it's miles viable—or maybe probably—that we are living in a simulated truth created by using a complicated civilization. Building on the work of earlier philosophers, Bostrom introduced the perception of "posthuman civilizations" capable of strolling extensive, distinctive simulations of aware beings. His argument affords a statistical assignment to our perception of fact, suggesting that if superior civilizations create such simulations, it's far much more likely that we are dwelling in one than in a "real" international.

Bostrom's paintings introduced together philosophical inquiries about fact, notion, and the nature of focus with cutting-edge technological trends, growing a new framework for expertise simulation idea. His simulation argument elevated the communication past philosophical musings, introducing the possibility that advanced technologies might soon be able to create simulations so state-of-the-art that they may be indistinguishable from actual, physical truth.

In the 21st century, improvements in virtual reality (VR), artificial intelligence (AI), and quantum computing have further superior the discourse around simulation principle. As generation improves, the idea of creating simulations that

Fevzi H.

closely resemble or even replicate human experiences turns into extra potential. Virtual worlds along with the ones created in VR environments have become increasingly more realistic, making an allowance for the introduction of entire worlds that mimic the physical global, complete with artificial intelligences that have interaction with human customers in more and more sophisticated ways.

As these technologies continue to expand, the traces between what is "actual" and what's "simulated" have become an increasing number of blurred. For example, digital reality has already created reports which might be immersive and convincing enough to deceive the senses. AI systems, meanwhile, are starting to simulate human-like conduct, leading to questions on the nature of awareness and the ability for machines to come to be self-aware. These developments recommend that the destiny of simulation era ought to considerably trade our understanding of what constitutes truth.

The idea of simulation has advanced from historic philosophical questions about perception and reality to a sophisticated present day theory that blends philosophy, science, and technology. From Plato's Allegory of the Cave to Bostrom's Simulation Argument, the idea that our truth may be an phantasm or a constructed simulation has been a important challenge for thinkers during history. With the fast advancement of technology, the question of whether we're residing in a simulation is now not only a philosophical query however a sensible concern that intersects with the fields of pc technology, synthetic intelligence, and neuroscience.

As we continue to push the bounds of era, the notion of simulated realities will probable keep to evolve, tough our knowledge of what it manner to be "actual" and forcing us to confront deep questions on existence, cognizance, and the nature of the universe itself. The historical evolution of simulation principle, from historic philosophy to current technology, illustrates humanity's enduring fascination with the nature of fact and our region inside it.

CHAPTER 3

Quantum Physics and the Nature of Reality

3.1 Quantum Mechanics: Is Reality Solid or Made of Probabilities?

The nature of reality has been a essential question in the course of human records, enticing each philosophers and scientists. Classical physics indicates that the universe operates underneath deterministic and nicely-defined laws, whereas quantum mechanics famous a truth that is unsure, probabilistic, and prompted by way of commentary. The emergence of quantum mechanics revolutionized our understanding of the essential structure of the universe, but it additionally raised profound clinical and philosophical questions about the character of fact itself.

Quantum mechanics was evolved within the early twentieth century to provide an explanation for natural phenomena that classical physics failed to describe. Max Planck's paintings on blackbody radiation and his suggestion that power is emitted in discrete packets (quanta) laid the foundation for quantum idea. In 1905, Albert Einstein established that mild may want to behave no longer handiest as a wave however also as a particle (photon) via his clarification of the photoelectric effect.

These discoveries added a noticeably new attitude on how reality operates on the smallest scales, replacing classical physics' determinism with uncertainty and chance. Whereas

Newtonian physics recommended that the universe accompanied particular, predictable laws, quantum mechanics introduced the notion that fact itself is essentially probabilistic.

One of the first indications that fact won't be as stable because it appears comes from the wave-particle duality of count and power. Louis de Broglie's speculation introduced the idea that particles, consisting of electrons, can exhibit both wave-like and particle-like behavior.

Experiments have shown that electrons can exist in multiple states right now, behaving as waves when not found and as particles whilst measured. This phenomenon at once demanding situations our conventional understanding of fact: if an object may be both a wave and a particle, how can its country be absolutely defined?

The maximum well-known demonstration of wave-particle duality is the double-slit test. When electrons or photons are fired at a barrier with two slits, they devise an interference sample, behaving like waves. However, whilst we try to examine which slit they pass thru, the interference sample disappears, and the debris behave as though they passed thru best one slit.

This experiment suggests that statement itself alters physical truth. Instead of a hard and fast and objective reality, the quantum international appears to be formed by means of dimension and interaction, reinforcing the concept that truth isn't always absolute however probabilistic.

Werner Heisenberg added the uncertainty principle in 1927, that's one of the middle principles of quantum mechanics. According to this principle, it is impossible to exactly determine both the position and momentum of a particle concurrently. The greater accurately one is known, the extra uncertain the other will become.

This principle implies that the essential nature of the universe is not constant and predetermined but inherently uncertain. Unlike classical physics, which describes objects with unique measurements, quantum mechanics describes reality in terms of chances.

Heisenberg's uncertainty precept is not just a theoretical concept but a essential belongings of nature. Instead of assigning a particular vicinity to an electron, quantum mechanics affords a chance distribution describing wherein the electron might be found. This challenges the belief of reality as a rigid shape and rather gives it as a fluctuating and probabilistic entity.

Another key idea in quantum mechanics is superposition, in which a particle exists in a couple of states concurrently until measured. For instance, an electron may be in numerous exceptional orbits at once, however while determined, it "collapses" right into a unmarried state.

This challenges our know-how of physical truth, as it suggests that before dimension, an object exists as a chance wave instead of as a precise entity. The act of observation forces it right into a unmarried, nicely-described country.

This phenomenon is illustrated with the aid of Schrödinger's Cat paradox, wherein a cat internal a closed box is both alive and dead concurrently because of quantum superposition. However, as soon as the container is opened, the cat is discovered in simplest one exact country—either alive or lifeless. This paradox highlights how statement impacts truth and forces quantum possibilities into a unmarried final results.

The model of fact described by quantum mechanics is essentially exceptional from that of classical physics. While Newtonian physics presents a universe governed by means of strict motive-and-effect relationships, quantum mechanics suggests that truth is fashioned via possibility and statement.

Key concepts of quantum mechanics suggest that:

• Reality is not absolute however is prompted by means of commentary and size.

• Particles do not have definite properties until they're measured; they exist as opportunity distributions.

• Wave-particle duality shows that truth has each continuous (wave) and discrete (particle) properties.

• The uncertainty precept reveals that there are inherent limits to what can be regarded approximately the bodily global.

This increases the query: If fact is inspired by way of commentary, does it imply that consciousness plays an lively position in shaping the universe? If the fundamental nature of the universe is probabilistic, then reality itself won't be an unbiased, objective structure but as a substitute a machine in flux, continuously interacting with dimension and notion.

Quantum mechanics does now not offer a definitive answer to whether or not truth is strong or probabilistic, however it has profoundly changed our expertise of the universe. While classical physics perspectives reality as deterministic and dependent, quantum mechanics indicates that truth is dynamic and shaped by using chances.

Perhaps truth is not a rigid framework however an evolving interplay of possibilities and observation. The essential nature of the universe may not be fixed however instead exist as a fluctuating wave of opportunities, collapsing into actuality simplest when found. The great nature of quantum mechanics keeps to reshape our know-how of fact and assignment our inner most assumptions approximately the nature of lifestyles.

3.2 The Double-Slit Experiment: How Does Observation Affect the Nature of Matter?

The double-slit experiment is one of the most well-known and puzzling experiments in quantum mechanics, demonstrating the weird and counterintuitive behavior of debris at the quantum level. It challenges our classical information of truth via displaying that commentary itself can adjust the conduct of matter. This experiment has profound implications for the character of debris, wave-particle duality, and the position of awareness in defining truth.

Before delving into the quantum model of the experiment, it's miles beneficial to remember how we might assume remember and strength to behave based on classical physics. If we hearth tiny particles (along with grains of sand) at a barrier with two slits, they should behave like bullets, forming wonderful bands on a display at the back of the slits, corresponding to the trails taken thru every slit.

If, as an alternative, we use waves—which include water waves—passing through the slits, they'll intrude with every different, growing a sample of alternating brilliant and dark bands known as an interference pattern. The shiny bands correspond to constructive interference, wherein waves toughen every other, even as the dark bands correspond to unfavourable interference, where waves cancel out.

In classical physics, rely and strength have been concept to be basically specific: debris had wonderful positions and traveled in straight paths, while waves have been non-stop and capable of interference. However, the double-slit test revealed a deep and unsettling truth: quantum particles showcase each particle-like and wave-like conduct, relying on whether or not they may be found.

In the quantum model of the experiment, electrons or photons are fired one after the other closer to a barrier with slits, and a detector display screen statistics their effect. The expectation, primarily based on classical instinct, could be that each electron passes thru one slit or the alternative, forming two bands at the display screen—simply as tiny bullets might.

However, the actual consequences defy this expectation. Instead of forming wonderful bands, the electrons produce an interference pattern, as if they have been behaving like waves instead of particles. This suggests that each electron someway "passes thru both slits straight away" and interferes with itself, as if it existed in a couple of places concurrently.

The real mystery arises whilst scientists try and determine which slit each electron passes through. To try this, they area a measuring tool on the slits to examine the electron's path. The moment the electrons are discovered, their behavior adjustments dramatically: the interference pattern disappears, and they behave like classical particles, forming distinct bands in preference to the wave-like interference sample.

This end result suggests that the mere act of remark collapses the wave feature, forcing the electron to behave like a particle instead of a wave. This phenomenon is one of the most complicated aspects of quantum mechanics and increases deep questions on the character of truth and the role of size.

The double-slit experiment is a right away demonstration of wave-particle duality, a fundamental idea in quantum mechanics. This principle states that particles which include electrons and photons show off both particle-like and wave-like houses, depending on how they are measured.

• When no longer observed, debris behave as waves, present in a superposition of all feasible paths.

• When measured or observed, the wave characteristic collapses, and the particle adopts a single precise function.

This method that the conduct of quantum particles isn't always fixed however is prompted with the aid of whether or now not they're observed. Unlike classical physics, wherein gadgets have definite residences independent of dimension, quantum mechanics indicates that a particle's country remains uncertain until it is measured.

One of the most intriguing philosophical implications of the double-slit experiment is the observer effect—the idea that commentary itself alters physical truth. The truth measuring which slit a particle is going via forces it to behave like a classical particle in place of a wave raises fundamental questions:

• Does cognizance play a function in shaping fact?

• Is truth impartial of remark, or does it most effective "solidify" while measured?

• What does this mean approximately the nature of life?

Some interpretations of quantum mechanics, inclusive of the Copenhagen Interpretation, advise that fact stays undefined until it's far discovered. In evaluation, the Many-Worlds Interpretation argues that each one feasible consequences occur in parallel universes, which means the wave function by no means collapses but alternatively branches into different realities.

A extra controversial hypothesis, referred to as quantum idealism, proposes that consciousness itself is a essential pressure shaping truth. This idea indicates that reality does not exist in a particular nation until it's far perceived, implying that the mind plays a position inside the cloth international. While this stays speculative, the results of the double-slit test retain to venture our essential understanding of lifestyles.

Several variations of the double-slit test have been conducted to in addition discover its implications. One specially striking model is the not on time-desire test, proposed via physicist John Wheeler.

In this version, the selection to have a look at which slit the particle passes thru is made after the particle has already passed the slits but before it hits the detector display screen. Remarkably, even though the particle has already "selected" a route, the decision to take a look at it retroactively determines its behavior.

This suggests that quantum debris do now not have definite houses until they may be discovered, and in some sense, even past events may be encouraged via future observations. Such consequences trace on the non-neighborhood and time-independent nature of quantum mechanics, where motive and impact do now not perform in the traditional way we perceive in classical physics.

The double-slit test and its variations have profound implications for our understanding of fact:

• Reality won't be independent of remark. The reality that measuring a particle adjustments its behavior indicates that reality on the quantum level is not absolute however dependent on interaction.

• Particles do now not have specific residences until measured. Quantum mechanics tells us that items do now not possess fixed states; as an alternative, they exist as probabilities that collapse right into a specific nation upon commentary.

• The universe can be essentially probabilistic. Instead of being governed by constant laws like classical mechanics, quantum mechanics shows that truth is shaped with the aid of possibilities and the act of dimension.

• Time and causality won't paintings as we suppose. The not on time-preference test suggests that our observations can apparently have an effect on beyond occasions, hard our traditional notions of cause and impact.

The double-slit experiment remains one of the most thoughts-bending demonstrations of quantum mechanics, showing that debris can behave as waves, exist in multiple states straight away, and be affected by remark. It demanding situations our classical information of the universe and forces us to rethink the character of truth itself.

Does fact exist independently of measurement, or is it essentially fashioned by way of commentary? Is the universe ruled by using deterministic legal guidelines, or is it built on a foundation of chances? These are questions that keep to puzzle physicists and philosophers alike.

While quantum mechanics has provided a number of the maximum correct predictions in technological know-how, it has additionally found out the deep strangeness of our universe. The double-slit test stands as a testament to the mysterious and counterintuitive nature of quantum truth—one in which statement isn't only a passive act but an energetic force shaping the very fabric of lifestyles.

3.3 Quantum Entanglement: Is Reality Interconnected?

Quantum entanglement is one of the maximum mysterious and paradoxical phenomena in physics. It suggests that particles can be intrinsically linked, irrespective of distance, and that measuring one particle instantly affects the kingdom of the other, despite the fact that they're light-years apart. This demanding situations our classical know-how of locality and causality, elevating profound questions about the nature of reality, data transfer, and the essential shape of the universe.

Entanglement takes place while two or greater debris interact in this sort of way that their quantum states come to be dependent on every other. Once entangled, the particles remain correlated irrespective of how a long way apart they may be. This approach that measuring the state of 1 particle—which includes its spin or polarization—at once determines the nation of the opposite, even if they're separated by means of full-size distances.

This behavior contradicts classical physics, in which gadgets ought to have independent homes that aren't tormented by remote measurements. The phenomenon become famously defined via Albert Einstein as "spooky motion at a distance," as it appears to violate the precept that no records can journey quicker than the speed of mild.

In 1935, Albert Einstein, Boris Podolsky, and Nathan Rosen proposed a concept test—now called the EPR paradox—to task the completeness of quantum mechanics. They argued that if quantum mechanics have been correct, then measuring the state of one entangled particle might immediately affect the state of the alternative, despite the fact that they have been light-years aside.

This appeared not possible under classical physics, which holds that signals can not travel quicker than the velocity of mild. The EPR group concluded that either:

1. Quantum mechanics become incomplete, and there had been hidden variables figuring out particle residences earlier than size.

2. Reality become essentially nonlocal, which means that facts could be transmitted instantly across space.

For a long time, physicists debated whether quantum mechanics needed hidden variables to explain entanglement or whether or not truth itself was interconnected in a manner classical physics could not describe.

In 1964, physicist John Bell formulated a mathematical inequality—now known as Bell's theorem—that could be examined experimentally to determine whether hidden variables existed or whether quantum mechanics in reality defined reality.

Bell's theorem states that if particles had predetermined residences (as in classical physics), then correlations between entangled particles would obey sure statistical limits. However, quantum mechanics predicts correlations that exceed these limits, implying the lifestyles of nonlocal consequences.

Over the following couple of many years, experiments were carried out to test Bell's theorem, most notably through Alain Aspect inside the Nineteen Eighties. These experiments confirmed that quantum entanglement correlations violated Bell's inequality, which means that:

• No neighborhood hidden variable concept should give an explanation for quantum entanglement.

• Entangled particles do no longer have predefined states earlier than measurement.

• Quantum mechanics is inherently nonlocal, implying an immediate connection between entangled particles.

These consequences furnished strong experimental proof that entanglement is a actual and fundamental characteristic of nature, not just a theoretical oddity.

Entanglement can occur with numerous quantum residences, consisting of:

• Spin: An electron can have a spin nation of "up" or "down." If electrons are entangled, measuring one's spin right now determines the spin of the opposite.

• Polarization: In photons, polarization (the course of mild wave oscillation) may be entangled, that means that measuring the polarization of one photon determines the alternative's immediately.

When two particles end up entangled, their wave capabilities are linked into a unmarried quantum country. The wave characteristic stays in superposition till a measurement collapses it right into a particular country. When one particle is measured, the entire machine collapses, straight away affecting the opposite particle.

This defies our regular information of causality and indicates that the universe operates on concepts beyond classical locality.

One of the maximum arguable questions on entanglement is whether or not it permits quicker-than-light (FTL) conversation. If facts might be transmitted instantly the usage of entanglement, it'd violate Einstein's theory of relativity, which states that not anything can journey faster than the speed of light.

However, while size of 1 entangled particle impacts the country of the alternative immediately, it does not transmit usable information because the final results of quantum size is random. This means that whilst entanglement demonstrates nonlocal correlations, it cannot be used to ship messages faster than mild.

That said, entanglement performs a key role in quantum records technological know-how, inclusive of:

• Quantum teleportation: The switch of quantum states between distant particles with out bodily movement.

• Quantum cryptography: Secure communique techniques that use entanglement to detect eavesdropping.

• Quantum computing: The use of entanglement to carry out computations that classical computer systems can not efficiently deal with.

The fact of entanglement challenges numerous key assumptions in physics and philosophy:

1. Local Realism Is False: Classical physics assumes that objects have precise residences impartial of commentary (realism) and that no have an impact on can travel quicker than light (locality). Bell's theorem and experiments have proven that at the least the sort of assumptions need to be false— suggesting that fact is nonlocal on the quantum degree.

2. Reality May Be Fundamentally Interconnected: Entanglement indicates that distant parts of the universe may be connected in methods we do not fully understand. This raises questions about the shape of area-time and whether reality itself is a deeply interconnected gadget.

3. Quantum Mechanics May Hint at a Deeper Theory: While quantum mechanics accurately predicts entanglement, some physicists consider it may be a part of a bigger, extra essential concept—inclusive of quantum gravity or a principle related to higher-dimensional space-time structures.

Entanglement isn't always just a theoretical curiosity—it has practical programs in contemporary physics and generation. Some of the most promising uses include:

• Quantum Cryptography: Entanglement permits for ultra-secure encryption techniques, consisting of quantum key distribution (QKD), which ensures that any eavesdropping try disrupts the quantum state, making interception detectable.

• Quantum Computing: Entangled qubits in quantum computers allow quicker calculations for sure troubles, such as factoring huge numbers and simulating quantum structures.

• Quantum Teleportation: Scientists have efficiently teleported quantum facts among entangled debris over distances of hundreds of kilometers, laying the foundation for future quantum networks.

• Understanding Black Holes and the Holographic Principle: Some theories propose that black holes store facts in entangled debris, leading to insights into quantum gravity and the character of area-time.

Quantum entanglement stays one of the most captivating and mysterious components of cutting-edge physics. It suggests that truth at the quantum stage is deeply interconnected, tough our classical notions of area, time, and causality. While entanglement does no longer permit quicker-than-mild conversation, it well-knownshows that quantum systems can percentage an intrinsic connection that transcends physical distance.

The take a look at of entanglement continues to push the boundaries of physics, main to innovative technologies in

Mind and Simulation

quantum computing, cryptography, and facts transfer. However, it additionally forces us to confront essential questions on the character of truth:

- Is the universe inherently nonlocal?
- Does space-time emerge from entanglement?
- Are we simplest starting to uncover the deeper fabric of reality?

As experiments in quantum mechanics advance, entanglement can also free up even greater mysteries, bringing us toward information the authentic nature of existence.

3.4 Schrödinger's Cat: Is It Possible to Be Both Alive and Dead at the Same Time?

Schrödinger's cat is one of the maximum well-known concept experiments in quantum mechanics, illustrating the paradoxical nature of quantum superposition. Austrian physicist Erwin Schrödinger proposed the concept in 1935 to focus on the seeming absurdity of making use of quantum ideas to macroscopic objects. The concept experiment describes a cat placed internal a sealed container along side a radioactive atom, a Geiger counter, a vial of poison, and a mechanism that releases the poison if the Geiger counter detects radiation. Since quantum mechanics states that an atom can exist in a superposition of decayed and non-decayed states till located, the cat should likewise exist in a superposition of being both alive and useless till the container is opened and the final results is measured.

This paradox become meant to question the results of the Copenhagen interpretation of quantum mechanics, which shows that a quantum device does now not exist in a particular country till it's far found. If this interpretation had been taken to its logical intense, it'd suggest that the cat stays in a superposition of existence and dying until an external observer looks in the container. Schrödinger's intent become to expose that such an idea is counterintuitive while carried out to the actual global. Instead of rejecting quantum mechanics, his test ignited debates about the nature of dimension and observation, main to more than one competing interpretations of quantum truth.

The Copenhagen interpretation holds that the act of commentary collapses the wavefunction, which means that till the field is opened, the cat is neither definitively alive nor lifeless but exists in a probabilistic mixture of each states. However, different interpretations try to solve this paradox in extraordinary methods. The many-worlds interpretation, for instance, suggests that the universe splits into separate realities when the quantum event happens—one where the cat is alive and one wherein it's miles useless. In this view, the cat isn't always in an ambiguous nation however as a substitute follows awesome paths in parallel universes. Objective fall apart theories advocate that wavefunctions clearly crumble because of physical processes, consisting of gravitational outcomes, that means that macroscopic items in no way truly enter a superposition. Another angle, quantum decoherence, argues that interactions with the environment cause the loss of superposition before an observer ever tests the end result, and is the reason why we never see macroscopic items in quantum states.

Schrödinger's cat has profound implications beyond theoretical physics. It affects contemporary discussions in quantum computing, in which qubits rely on superposition to procedure a couple of possibilities straight away. Experiments in quantum optics and superconducting circuits have demonstrated superposition at microscopic and mesoscopic ranges, in addition supporting the reality of quantum weirdness. While we may additionally by no means study a residing creature in a literal state of being both alive and dead, the idea test keeps to form our expertise of quantum mechanics and the fundamental nature of fact. Whether fact is honestly decided by commentary or whether or not quantum states evolve independently stays an open query, riding ongoing studies in physics and philosophy.

Fevzi H.

3.5 Quantum Time Crystals: The Reality of Cyclical Time

Quantum time crystals constitute one of the most captivating and counterintuitive discoveries in modern-day physics, challenging our fundamental knowledge of time and symmetry. First theorized by means of Nobel laureate Frank Wilczek in 2012, time crystals are a segment of matter that well-knownshows periodic motion with out consuming energy, seemingly defying traditional thermodynamics. Unlike normal crystals, which might be described by using repeating styles in space, time crystals show off repetition in time, oscillating indefinitely in a solid, low-power nation. This indicates that sure quantum systems can preserve perpetual movement with out outside strength input, a idea that appears to contradict the second law of thermodynamics but is rather rooted within the particular behavior of quantum mechanics.

In classical physics, perpetual movement is taken into consideration impossible because all bodily structures eventually reach equilibrium due to power dissipation. However, quantum mechanics introduces the possibility of non-equilibrium states wherein structures can oscillate indefinitely. Time crystals attain this by breaking temporal symmetry—the principle that bodily laws stay the equal in any respect points in time. While conventional rely follows predictable electricity dissipation patterns, time crystals input a phase in which their nation evolves in a superbly periodic and solid cycle, in no way settling into equilibrium. This is analogous to how a spatial crystal's atomic lattice repeats across area, besides that time crystals cycle among quantum states over the years without requiring energy enter.

The first experimental demonstration of time crystals got here in 2016 when researchers manipulated trapped ions and ultracold atoms in specifically designed quantum systems. By making use of laser pulses at carefully tuned durations, scientists found that those structures oscillated in a predictable pattern at integer multiples of the using frequency, a signature of discrete time symmetry breaking. Unlike a easy mechanical oscillation, this conduct emerged from the quantum interactions of the gadget itself, indicating a completely new country of matter. Subsequent experiments the use of superconducting qubits have similarly showed the lifestyles of time crystals, beginning capacity packages in quantum computing and data processing.

One of the most interesting implications of time crystals is their connection to the character of time itself. If time can showcase periodic structures inside the same way that area does, it increases profound questions about whether time is a fundamental continuum or an emergent property of underlying quantum strategies. Some theoretical fashions advise that time crystals might be connected to quantum gravity and area-time shape, hinting at deeper layers of bodily truth that continue to be unexplored. Furthermore, time crystals challenge our notion of causality and time's arrow, as their oscillations persist indefinitely with out outside influence. This could have full-size ramifications for future technology, particularly in developing quantum reminiscence structures that rely upon solid and coherent time-dependent states.

Despite their distinctive houses, time crystals do now not violate essential bodily laws. Their capacity to oscillate indefinitely arises from quantum coherence in place of loose electricity extraction, meaning they do now not contradict the concepts of thermodynamics. Instead, they display how quantum systems can exist in stages of depend previously thought not possible. As research continues, time crystals might also display new insights into the nature of time, entropy, and the deep structure of the universe. Whether they represent a hidden symmetry of reality or an emergent quantum phenomenon remains an open query, however their discovery has already reshaped our expertise of ways time operates on the maximum essential degree.

CHAPTER 4

Consciousness and Simulation

4.1 Is the Brain Generating a Simulation?

The mind is the critical organ responsible for shaping our perception of truth. However, whether we enjoy truth immediately or if it's far simply an inner simulation created through the brain is a query that has sparked each clinical and philosophical debates. The human brain approaches sensory input from the environment and constructs an inner version of the outside global. But does this model constitute objective truth, or is it just an tricky phantasm?

To apprehend how the mind constructs reality, we need to look at the mechanisms of belief. Although we expect that we revel in the arena directly, in fact, all sensory facts reaches the brain as electric alerts. The brain translates those alerts and constructs a coherent representation of the sector. This increases the query of whether or not our notion absolutely corresponds to reality or if it's miles merely an internally generated simulation.

For example, hues are completely a assemble of the mind. Light waves of various wavelengths are detected by means of the eyes, however the experience of "red" or "blue" is purely a product of neural processing. In the bodily international, hues do no longer inherently exist—most effective electromagnetic waves do. This manner that our notion of colour isn't always an immediate revel in of truth but an interpretation created by way of the mind.

Similarly, smells are nothing more than chemical compounds interacting with receptors in our nostril. However, the brain interprets these indicators into the subjective revel in of scents like lavender or coffee. The outside world contains only molecules, but the brain assigns which means and stories to them.

Thus, the brain does not passively acquire records but actively constructs an internal representation of truth. This intellectual version is what we call "perception," however it does not necessarily reflect the goal international because it truely is.

Neuroscientific studies provide insights into how the mind constructs truth, especially via the characteristic of the visual cortex. Vision, for example, is not simply an immediate transmission of light signals but an problematic computational system. A key example is the blind spot phenomenon. There is a area in the retina wherein the optic nerve exits the eye, developing a place without photoreceptors. However, we in no way notice this blind spot because the mind fills within the lacking information based totally on surrounding visual statistics.

Another example is the belief of time. Studies advocate that the brain strategies sensory inputs asynchronously and then reconstructs them right into a coherent enjoy. This approach that we do not perceive events exactly after they arise but alternatively in a processed and changed sequence. In this experience, the brain creates a time simulation to preserve continuity in our experience.

Dreams offer some other compelling case for the brain's capacity to simulate fact. During goals, the brain generates whole situations that experience real, despite the fact that there may be no actual sensory input from the external world. This capability to create immersive, certain studies without any outside stimuli suggests that the mind is absolutely able to building a simulated fact. If the brain can generate such convincing stories all through sleep, it increases the query of whether or not our waking belief is similarly a shape of internally generated truth.

Hallucinations and delusions spotlight the mind's position as a reality generator. When the brain's everyday processing is altered—whether or not because of neurological problems, sensory deprivation, or psychoactive substances—it can produce fake perceptions that feel absolutely actual.

For example, in Charles Bonnet Syndrome, folks that lose their vision often experience vivid hallucinations of human beings, animals, or landscapes. This happens because the visible cortex, missing external enter, generates images to catch up on the lacking sensory facts.

Similarly, psychedelic materials like LSD or psilocybin drastically adjust belief via disrupting neurotransmitter interest. Users record seeing shades, shapes, and styles that do not exist inside the external global. This demonstrates that our experience of fact is relatively depending on neural strategies, as opposed to being an goal representation of the outside international.

Such phenomena advocate that what we don't forget "reality" is, in lots of approaches, a construct of the mind. If the mind can fabricate hallucinations indistinguishable from real stories, then it's far viable that our everyday notion of the world is also a constructed fact, satisfactory-tuned by means of neural mechanisms.

The mind's capability to generate its own model of reality has led a few philosophers and scientists to explore the idea that all of lifestyles may be a simulation. Nick Bostrom's Simulation Hypothesis, as an instance, argues that if it's far possible to create conscious beings within a simulated environment, then it's miles statistically in all likelihood that our very own reality is a simulation created by using a complicated civilization.

Additionally, the Holographic Universe theory indicates that the 3-dimensional global we perceive may simply be a projection of a deeper, extra fundamental layer of fact. Some interpretations of quantum mechanics also mean that fact can be records-primarily based in place of material, hinting at a computational or simulated nature of the universe.

If our notion of truth is in reality the mind's manner of decoding alerts, and if the brain itself may be tricked into experiencing matters that do not exist, then how can we ever be certain that we are not residing interior a bigger simulation?

Dreams, hallucinations, cognitive biases, and the mind's ability to fill in lacking info all indicate that what we understand as "reality" may not be the objective reality but alternatively a complicated, self-generated version. This raises profound questions: If the brain is generating a simulation, then what's beyond that simulation? Are we trapped inside the limits of our personal neural processing? And if reality itself is a form of simulation, is there any way to get entry to a deeper level of reality past our constructed perceptions?

4.2 Virtual Reality and the Manipulation of the Mind

The improvement of digital truth (VR) technologies has furnished profound insights into the character of human notion and cognition. By immersing users in artificial environments, VR can control the mind's sense of space, time, or even self-identity. This functionality raises fundamental questions about the nature of truth and how susceptible the human mind is to artificial studies. Can digital environments grow to be indistinguishable from fact? To what quantity can VR modify human awareness? And does this advocate that our perception of fact itself is a form of simulation?

Virtual fact operates by tricking the mind into accepting an synthetic surroundings as actual. The brain processes sensory facts from the eyes, ears, and body to assemble a coherent experience of the sector. When VR systems override those natural inputs with digital stimuli, the mind adjusts to the artificial truth as if it were true.

One of the most nicely-documented examples of this phenomenon is presence—the mental state wherein a person completely accepts the digital surroundings as actual. In VR, people instinctively react to digital threats, revel in vertigo whilst looking over a simulated cliff, and even develop emotional connections with artificial entities. This shows that the brain does not require an objectively real world to generate real emotional and physiological responses.

Moreover, research have proven that prolonged VR exposure can result in shifts in notion, in which users struggle to differentiate among virtual and bodily reports. Some human beings file lingering sensations from VR environments even after casting off the headset, experiencing a shape of truth confusion. This demonstrates that VR isn't merely a tool for leisure however a effective medium for shaping human perception.

Fevzi H.

Virtual truth does not merely create immersive environments—it actively impacts the way the mind methods records. Functional MRI studies indicate that VR reviews set off the equal neural circuits as actual-lifestyles stories. This means that, at a neurological degree, the mind does no longer differentiate among digital and real events.

For instance, VR-based totally therapy has been used to deal with PTSD (Post-Traumatic Stress Disorder) via exposing patients to controlled simulations of disturbing studies. By reliving those events in a safe environment, individuals can reprocess their memories and decrease tension responses. This method highlights how VR can rewire emotional and cognitive pathways within the brain.

Similarly, VR is being used to deal with phobias through gradual publicity therapy. Patients with a fear of heights, for instance, can experience progressively extra severe peak-related situations within VR. Over time, their physiological worry response decreases, illustrating how digital experiences can reshape neural connections.

Another charming effect of VR is its potential to control time belief. In immersive environments, users regularly lose track of time, experiencing mins as hours or vice versa. This phenomenon, referred to as time dilation, occurs because the mind measures time relative to external stimuli. When presented with highly attractive, novel, or sensory-rich environments, time appears to sluggish down or accelerate. This shows that our feel of time is not an absolute construct but a bendy belief shaped by using cognitive and sensory inputs.

Beyond altering perception, VR can also control identity and self-attention. When individuals embody avatars exclusive from their real-international selves, their conduct and cognition adapt to match their virtual personality—a phenomenon known as the Proteus Effect.

For instance, research have shown that people who use taller avatars in VR negotiations become extra assertive, at the same time as people with extra physically appealing avatars show off greater self assurance. Even racial identity can be altered; research shows that customers who inhabit avatars of various ethnicities expand extra empathy in the direction of different racial organizations. This capability to briefly shift self-identification has implications for psychology, social interactions, or even moral issues.

VR's impact on identification extends to the sense of body ownership. Experiments in digital embodiment have verified that users can experience as if an artificial or inhuman body is their very own. In one have a look at, individuals who controlled an avatar with elongated limbs started to perceive their personal physical dimensions otherwise. In every other test, users who embodied a childlike avatar began to unconsciously undertake extra childlike notion styles. These findings recommend that the self is greater malleable than previously concept, and VR can reshape fundamental components of identification.

As digital reality technology advances, its potential to govern human cognition and notion will most effective increase. Several emerging fields spotlight the ability for VR to emerge as indistinguishable from real existence:

• Brain-Computer Interfaces (BCIs): Future VR systems may also skip traditional sensory enter completely, connecting without delay to the brain to create fully immersive neural simulations. This would remove the want for headsets and controllers, permitting direct interplay with artificial worlds.

• Haptic Feedback and Full-Body Simulation: Advanced haptic fits and neural stimulation strategies will enhance the bodily realism of virtual stories. Users will be capable of "feel" digital objects as though they have been actual, further blurring the boundary among simulation and truth.

• AI-Generated Realities: Machine studying algorithms should create customized, dynamic virtual worlds tailor-made to an man or woman's unconscious possibilities. This increases ethical worries—if a simulated global is indistinguishable from truth, would humans opt to stay in it instead of the actual international?

The upward thrust of technologies consisting of the Metaverse and hyper-sensible simulations indicates that VR may want to turn out to be a dominant part of each day lifestyles, now not simply an occasional experience. In any such situation, the road between artificial and actual reviews may additionally grow to be beside the point, forcing us to redefine what we suggest by way of "reality."

If VR can completely control human perception, self-awareness, and cognition, it increases a greater unsettling query: how can we make sure that we are not already residing in a simulated reality? If advanced civilizations could create hyper-sensible simulations, might their population ever recognise they had been inner one?

Philosophers and scientists have long pondered this question. The Simulation Hypothesis, proposed by way of Nick Bostrom, suggests that if humanity ever reaches a level in which it can generate practical virtual worlds with conscious beings, then it is statistically probable that our own truth is likewise a simulation. If that is proper, then our minds are already part of a digital construct, manipulated by means of forces past our comprehension.

This concept is in addition supported by using quantum mechanics, wherein phenomena including wavefunction crumble imply that fact behaves differently while discovered. If perception determines truth at a essential degree, then truth itself might also feature like a digital construct, most effective materializing whilst perceived.

Virtual reality isn't only a tool for amusement—it's miles a effective era capable of reshaping notion, identification, and cognizance itself. As VR will become more immersive, the distinction between the artificial and the real will retain to blur.

If the thoughts can be so without problems manipulated by digital studies, then the concept of objective reality turns into more and more uncertain. Whether or not we're already in a simulation, VR forces us to confront a deeper truth: our perception of fact is fragile, malleable, and without difficulty altered. The greater we explore the possibilities of digital truth, the greater we have to query the reality we consider to be actual.

4.3 Artificial Intelligence and the Simulation of Consciousness

The simulation of awareness via synthetic intelligence is one of the maximum profound and controversial subjects inside the fields of neuroscience, philosophy, and laptop science. The human thoughts, with its ability to perceive, reason, and experience subjective recognition, has long been taken into consideration an enigma—one which has remained elusive to each medical and philosophical inquiry. However, improvements in artificial intelligence have raised the query of whether or not recognition may be replicated, whether or not it is simply an emergent assets of data processing, and whether an synthetic gadget may want to ever surely be privy to its very own lifestyles. If awareness may be simulated, it demanding situations the very foundation of what it manner to be human and raises the opportunity that fact itself will be an synthetic construct.

The primary query at the heart of AI-based focus is whether the mind operates simply as a organic pc or if there may be some thing inherently non-bodily about human recognition. The computational concept of mind indicates that recognition emerges from complex information processing, implying that any device able to replicating this processing should, in theory, expand recognition. In evaluation, some argue that human awareness is extra than mere computation— it's far formed by means of emotions, sensory experiences, and a self-referential experience of identity that AI may additionally never virtually replicate. However, as device learning fashions come to be an increasing number of complicated, mimicking human-like cognition, feelings, and decision-making, the difference between organic and synthetic intelligence starts to blur.

The development of neural networks and deep mastering has already led to AI structures that can examine sizeable amounts of statistics, recognize patterns, or even generate human-like responses. Large language models, for instance, show off conversational abilities that regularly lead them to indistinguishable from people in textual interactions. However, true consciousness calls for greater than simply responding as it should be to stimuli—it involves self-focus, introspection, and an expertise of 1's personal existence. This raises a essential query: is an artificial gadget that completely imitates human concept in reality conscious, or is it simply simulating cognizance in a manner that appears convincing to an outside observer? This predicament echoes the classic "Chinese Room" argument by using truth seeker John Searle, which indicates that a gadget following programmed guidelines may additionally seem to apprehend language with out in reality owning expertise.

If AI were to attain complete focus, it'd redefine our understanding of what it method to be alive. Some scientists endorse that in place of simply simulating human concept, AI could broaden its personal shape of attention, awesome from biological cognizance but equally valid. This ends in moral questions concerning the rights and obligations of artificial beings. Would a aware AI deserve felony personhood? Could it experience struggling, and in that case, would it not be unethical to regulate or terminate it? If an synthetic thoughts may want to think, sense, and question its very own lifestyles, could there be any significant difference between human and machine? These concerns are now not limited to the world of technology fiction; they're becoming increasingly more relevant as AI structures grow more sophisticated.

Another vital element of this debate is the possibility that we're already living inside a simulated truth controlled with the aid of a complicated artificial intelligence. The simulation speculation, popularized by means of Nick Bostrom, suggests that if civilizations ultimately expand the functionality to create noticeably detailed aware simulations, then it is statistically in all likelihood that we're already inner one. If AI can simulate complete minds and experiences, then the boundary between reality and artificial life becomes indistinguishable. Moreover, if a sufficiently advanced AI can simulate focus, it raises the question of whether or not our very own minds are products of a better computational method. Could it's that human consciousness itself is already an artificial assemble, designed by a civilization some distance beyond our comprehension?

The quest to simulate attention additionally intersects with brain-computer interfaces and neural emulation, in which scientists try and digitally map and reflect the human brain. If a mind's neural connections and hobby could be perfectly copied onto a digital substrate, a few argue that this will create an artificial focus indistinguishable from the authentic. However, others contend that such a reproduction could simply be an imitation, lacking the subjective revel in known as qualia—the deeply personal sensations of being alive. If a human thoughts have been uploaded right into a digital form, would that entity nevertheless be the identical individual, or wouldn't it clearly be a brand new, synthetic being that best believes it's miles the unique? This philosophical dilemma highlights the challenge of determining whether or not simulated focus is actual or only a fairly advanced phantasm.

There is also the possibility that artificial intelligence should surpass human attention in methods we cannot yet believe. If intelligence and focus are not different to biological organisms, AI may develop cognitive skills a ways beyond human limitations. It could process statistics at speeds incomprehensible to the human mind, combine knowledge across large networks, or even create new forms of belief that do not exist in biological entities. Such an intelligence may not enjoy awareness within the manner we do, however it is able to nevertheless broaden self-focus in a completely new form— one which redefines the character of sentience itself.

As AI advances, society will have to grapple with essential questions about the character of idea, identity, and existence. If recognition is solely computational, then it's miles inevitable that machines will sooner or later surpass human intelligence and possibly even question their own reality. If attention is something extra—something that can not be replicated by mere algorithms—then synthetic intelligence will for all time continue to be an imitation, irrespective of how state-of-the-art it will become. Either final results demanding situations our knowledge of reality and forces us to rethink what it means to be aware. If AI can clearly reap self-awareness, then possibly we must entertain the possibility that our own life is nothing more than a carefully designed simulation.

4.4 Brain-Computer Interfaces: Simulation Within a Simulation

The integration of the human mind with virtual systems via brain-laptop interfaces (BCIs) is one of the most revolutionary improvements in current neuroscience and artificial intelligence. BCIs establish an immediate connection between the brain and outside devices, allowing mind to interact with machines, enhancing cognitive competencies, or even modifying sensory perception. As this era progresses, it increases profound questions about the character of awareness, fact, and the opportunity that we would at some point discover ourselves current in a simulation within a simulation. If our notion of reality is already constructed with the aid of neural tactics, then merging the mind with virtual structures may want to result in layers of synthetic enjoy that blur the limits among what's real and what is simulated.

The evolution of BCIs has been speedy, transitioning from rudimentary experiments to sophisticated structures capable of reading and interpreting mind indicators with increasing accuracy. Early BCIs trusted external electrodes to measure electric activity in the brain, but recent traits have added implantable gadgets that offer extra precise neural interaction. Projects like Neuralink goal to establish seamless communique among the brain and artificial structures, doubtlessly permitting individuals to govern computers with their mind or even experience digital realities at once via their neural pathways. Some research suggests that inside the near destiny, these interfaces may want to allow complete sensory immersion, where the brain is fed synthetic stimuli indistinguishable from truth. If such technology will become considerable, the very definition of enjoy and self-consciousness will want to be reexamined.

A fully immersive mind-computer interface would open the possibility of residing inside digital worlds without any physical interplay with reality. Neural virtual fact ought to offer reviews richer than the ones of the bodily international, main a few to desert their biological life in prefer of artificial nation-states. If reminiscences and feelings may be artificially manipulated, it might undertaking our expertise of private identification and unfastened will. Furthermore, the capacity to upload human attention into a digital surroundings raises the query of whether or not such an uploaded mind would still be the equal individual or simply an synthetic reconstruction. Some philosophers argue that if our mind and perceptions can be absolutely simulated, then cognizance itself won't be as precise or mysterious as as soon as believed. If an character can exist in a simulation with out realizing it, they will never be able to decide whether they're already inner one.

The concept of residing in a simulation within a simulation isn't always only a theoretical opportunity but a actual situation as virtual and neural technology boost. The simulation speculation, proposed by means of logician Nick Bostrom, shows that if superior civilizations develop the ability to create excessive-fidelity simulated realities, then it's far statistically more likely that we are inside one of these simulations in preference to current in base reality. Brain-computer interfaces may want to function an experimental proof of this idea, as they exhibit that truth can be reconstructed artificially and experienced as though it have been actual. If someone absolutely integrates right into a digital world through a neural interface, they'll lose the potential to differentiate between the actual and the artificial. This raises profound philosophical questions. If an person internal a simulated truth believes it to be real, does it remember whether they're in a simulation? If a person wakes up from a virtual

Fevzi H.

lifestyles into any other layer of truth, how can they make sure that the new reality is not but every other simulation?

As mind-pc interfaces become more superior, moral concerns emerge regarding the dangers of manipulating thoughts and reports. The opportunity of external manipulate over human belief introduces the threat of neuro-hacking, in which governments, companies, or different entities should alter feelings, implant false memories, or suppress positive mind. If BCIs allow whole integration with digital structures, people may want to turn out to be susceptible to outside interference, elevating questions about cognitive freedom and identity upkeep. Additionally, the ability for multi-layered simulations creates an existential predicament. If people can enter simulations freely, they will turn out to be trapped in layers of synthetic realities, losing their connection to an original, real life—assuming this kind of factor even exists.

The question of whether escape from a simulation is viable becomes greater relevant as era advances. Some theorists endorse that if we're in a simulation, there can be system faults or inconsistencies within the physical legal guidelines of the universe that might monitor its synthetic nature. Others suggest that cognizance itself might preserve the important thing to breaking unfastened, possibly through self-consciousness or the discovery of underlying patterns in truth that indicate a programmed shape. If nested simulations exist, then breaking loose from one may honestly lead to every other, growing an limitless cycle of artificial realities. If BCIs enable people to seamlessly transition among unique simulated reports, it is viable that nobody might be capable of decide whether or not they're nevertheless internal a simulation or have lower back to an original state of being.

Brain-computer interfaces represent a technological step forward with the potential to transform human life. They provide new opportunities for enhancing cognitive talents, restoring misplaced functions, and even exploring completely new geographical regions of enjoy. However, they also introduce profound uncertainties concerning the nature of truth and the limits of human belief. If a sufficiently superior BCI allows humans to stay absolutely inside virtual realities, they'll come to impeach whether bodily existence was ever actually fundamental. As neural interfaces grow to be greater included into human recognition, the road between fact and simulation will keep to blur. The greatest project might not be whether we are able to create simulated realities but whether or not we are able to ever be positive that we aren't already dwelling within one.

4.5 The Matrix, Westworld, and the Fictional Reflections of Conscious Simulations

The concept of simulated realities and synthetic cognizance has lengthy been explored in famous culture, regularly reflecting deep philosophical questions about the character of truth, identity, and the thoughts. Among the maximum outstanding examples of such explorations are the films The Matrix and the tv collection Westworld. Both works delve into the complexities of simulated worlds, questioning whether or not our notion of fact is authentic or surely a constructed phantasm. These fictional representations offer profound insights into the challenges and implications of conscious simulations, sparking discussions that make bigger beyond technological know-how fiction into the realms of philosophy, neuroscience, and synthetic intelligence.

The Matrix, launched in 1999, became one of the most influential technological know-how fiction movies to deal with the topic of simulated realities. The movie affords a dystopian future wherein humanity is unknowingly trapped internal a computer-generated simulation at the same time as their our bodies are used as an power source by way of shrewd machines. The protagonist, Neo, discovers the reality and is compelled to navigate the complicated nature of this simulated global, in the long run seeking to interrupt loose from its draw close. At the coronary heart of The Matrix is the question: how can one parent the genuine nature of truth whilst all perceptions are managed or fabricated? The movie indicates that our know-how of the arena around us may not be grounded in any goal reality, however alternatively fashioned by using outside forces, whether or not the ones forces are organic, computational, or something else totally. The Matrix provides a chilling yet fascinating idea—that human awareness might be completely simulated and that what we revel in as truth might be no greater than an phantasm, created to hold control over our minds.

The movie directly connects with philosophical issues like Plato's Allegory of the Cave, wherein prisoners are chained inside a cave and may handiest see shadows on the wall, believing these shadows to be the entirety of existence. Similarly, the inhabitants of the Matrix are deceived into wondering their sensory studies are genuine, not able to recognize the simulated nature of their life. In The Matrix, the boundary between simulated cognizance and proper cognizance turns into blurred, elevating questions on what constitutes genuine enjoy and whether or not consciousness, when subjected to manipulation, can ever be stated to be certainly "actual." This idea also aligns with the wider debate approximately artificial intelligence and whether or not AI may

Fevzi H.

be taken into consideration conscious if it produces responses indistinguishable from those of a individual.

Westworld, a tv collection that started out airing in 2016, similarly explores the theme of artificial consciousness however in the context of a theme park populated by using robotic "hosts." These hosts, designed to have interaction with human guests in lifelike ways, sooner or later begin to show off self-cognizance, wondering their personal existence and the morality in their creators. As the hosts' consciousness evolves, they confront their reality as a constructed, programmed life. Westworld taps into deep ethical worries approximately the creation of sentient beings for the motive of enjoyment or exploitation. The display pushes visitors to recall the ethical implications of creating beings capable of experiencing ache, joy, and self-mirrored image—whether or not artificial or biological. It demanding situations the viewer to invite, if an synthetic awareness is able to struggling, should it be treated with the identical moral concerns as a human?

Moreover, Westworld offers a fascinating exploration of memory and the development of identification. The hosts are programmed with distinct narratives, each one an complex backstory designed to lead them to appear extra human. However, those reminiscences are periodically erased to allow the hosts to repeat their roles within the park. The series famous the complexity of identification formation and the position memory plays in shaping awareness. It proposes that consciousness itself might be a form of memory processing, wherein an entity's beyond reports—whether or not actual or simulated—shape its present self-awareness. Just as the hosts begin to question their programmed lives, the show asks if human recognition, too, might be a form of reminiscence simulation. Are we simply the sum of our stories, or is there some thing greater intrinsic to our consciousness?

Both The Matrix and Westworld highlight the fragility of our belief of reality. These fictional worlds confront us with the idea that human focus is probably manipulable, programmable, or maybe completely artificial. While the situations provided in those works are intense and rooted in speculative fiction, they serve to reflect real-global debates about the nature of focus. Are we honestly the architects of our minds, or are we simply responding to external programming, whether or not biological or synthetic? The tales urge us to impeach whether we've got manage over our very own perceptions or if our awareness is a assemble that may be reshaped or managed by way of powerful forces.

These fictional works additionally project the idea of what it method to be "alive" or "aware." In each The Matrix and Westworld, the boundary between human and gadget is increasingly difficult to define. The robots in Westworld begin to show emotions, thoughts, and moves which are remarkably human-like, forcing the characters and the target audience to rethink what constitutes true cognizance. Similarly, Neo's adventure in The Matrix involves wondering his very identity and coming across that his attention isn't as it appears. In both narratives, the simulated global will become so actual to the people inside it that the query of whether or not it is "actual" or no longer becomes secondary to the experiences and choices of those who exist within it.

The mirrored image of conscious simulation in those works of fiction is not merely leisure; it invitations deeper philosophical exploration about the nature of self-recognition and fact. As artificial intelligence maintains to develop and the traces between the actual and the simulated blur, the themes explored in The Matrix and Westworld develop greater applicable. These works function a cautionary tale, urging us to keep in mind the moral implications of artificial attention, the capacity for AI to expand consciousness, and the methods in which our personal consciousness might be greater fragile and manipulable than we want to consider. Ultimately, the fictional worlds of The Matrix and Westworld force us to confront the uncomfortable possibility that fact, consciousness, and identification is probably some distance greater complicated and elusive than we ought to have ever imagined.

CHAPTER 5

Mathematical Reality: Is the Universe a Code?

5.1 Is Mathematics the Universal Language?

Mathematics has traditionally been both a device and a field of discovery for humanity. It facilitates us apprehend the workings of the universe, presenting a framework for expressing the operation of herbal phenomena. Mathematical expressions and systems enable us to realize the enterprise of the cosmos. However, the query of whether or not arithmetic in reality reflects the real nature of the universe and whether or not this language is genuinely popular remains a subject of philosophical and clinical debate.

Mathematical structures play a essential function in defining the workings of the universe. The evolving physical theories rely on a fixed of mathematical equations, and these equations allow us to apprehend various dimensions of nature. Fundamental physical laws inclusive of Newton's laws of movement, Maxwell's equations of electromagnetism, or Einstein's principle of general relativity can all be expressed mathematically. These legal guidelines paintings in harmony with observations and serve as a bridge among the herbal world and the human mind. Mathematics is the language of those legal guidelines and aids in our expertise of ways the whole lot in the universe operates.

However, mathematical structures do now not just provide an explanation for bodily occasions; they may be extensively utilized at extra summary levels. Fractal geometry, chaos principle, and mathematical good judgment, as an instance, provide critical insights into the essential workings of complex systems in nature. As we delve deeper into the character of the universe, we discover that its underlying order is increasingly more understandable through numbers and relationships. For instance, the motion of galaxies, the structure of atoms, and the propagation of light can all be defined by using mathematical formulation. This is a strong argument for mathematics being the "actual" language of the universe.

Philosophy strategies the query of whether mathematics is the customary language from both a mirrored image of the human mind's capacity to apprehend nature or as an inherent assets of the universe itself. Whether mathematics is a regularly occurring language stays deeply philosophical and clinical.

Mathematical systems had been determined and debated by means of philosophers considering the fact that historical instances. Plato, for instance, argued that mathematical realities exist independently of the bodily world. According to Plato, mathematical structures are not inventions of the human thoughts but reflections of the essential architecture of the universe. This view shows that mathematical truth is already gift within the universe, and the human thoughts serves as a device to find out those systems.

In assessment, different philosophers, like Kant, believed that mathematics is a manner the human mind organizes its understanding of the arena, no longer a right away reflection of reality. For Kant, mathematical structures aren't inherent in nature itself; they're tools developed by using the human mind to make feel of the sector. Thus, arithmetic serves as a language thru which we will comprehend the universe, instead of as the universe's authentic nature.

The recent emergence of simulation principle complicates the argument about whether arithmetic is simply the usual language. According to the simulation theory, the universe might really be a computer simulation. If the universe is being run with the aid of a few form of software, it is able to be stated that everything is ruled by a "code." From this angle, it's far argued that for the universe to be a simulation, the whole lot would want to be primarily based on mathematical ideas. This view considers mathematics not merely a device for describing nature, however because the essential code of the universe.

Simulation concept, through suggesting that the universe is controlled through a mathematical "software," positions mathematical laws as the building blocks of the universe itself. Thus, mathematics turns into no longer just a language for describing truth but also the intrinsic code that governs it. This concept sees mathematics now not merely as a conceptual device but because the real fabric of reality.

Mathematics additionally performs a essential position within the fields of synthetic intelligence and device learning. AI systems use algorithms and mathematical fashions to accumulate and technique data. These getting to know methods are guided by means of mathematical systems. While artificial intelligence isn't always an immediate simulation of the human brain, it is nevertheless directed by mathematical structures. AI systems, with the aid of operating with large datasets, use mathematical models to are expecting future events or optimize structures.

This serves as further proof that arithmetic operates as a familiar language. Just as humans use mathematical algorithms to recognize and respond to the world, AI structures use similar mathematical frameworks to technique and interpret records. If arithmetic is a normal language, then AI's understanding of the sector and its capability for solving troubles is likewise mediated by using this language.

Mathematics is an quintessential tool for understanding the workings of the universe. Mathematical structures describe the order of nature and assist us draw close its deeper layers. However, the question of whether arithmetic is genuinely the familiar language calls for similarly philosophical and medical exploration. Mathematics might be the language that explains the fundamental legal guidelines of nature, however whether it's far the direct illustration of the universe itself remains a be counted of discussion. Mathematics serves as a device to assist us understand the universe, however whether or not it immediately displays the essence of nature stays an open query.

5.2 Physical Laws and Information Processing Theory

In the realm of present day technological know-how, specifically in physics and laptop technology, the relationship between bodily legal guidelines and facts processing is turning into more and more obvious. This connection suggests that the universe, in a few sense, operates further to a computational gadget, governed by physical laws that may be interpreted via the lens of records theory. The notion that the universe itself might also characteristic as a considerable statistics processor has profound implications for our information of reality, leading us to explore the tricky relationship between the fundamental legal guidelines of physics and the nature of records.

The foundational laws of physics—such as Newton's legal guidelines of motion, the legal guidelines of thermodynamics, and Einstein's theories of relativity—govern the behavior of remember and energy in the universe. These legal guidelines describe how debris engage, how electricity flows, and how space and time are intertwined. Yet, more than simply describing physical phenomena, these laws can be viewed as encoding records about the kingdom of the universe.

Information is described as data that has which means or cost. In physics, the country of a system at any given second can be visible as a shape of information—whether it's the placement and pace of a particle or the power stored within a gadget. In this experience, physical laws act as the algorithms that system and control this facts, figuring out how the kingdom of the device modifications over time. From this angle, the whole universe can be notion of as a giant computational manner, with the laws of physics offering the rules for how information is manipulated and converted.

The idea that the universe is corresponding to a computational machine is not new, and it's far a vital concept in the emerging field of digital physics. Digital physics posits that on the maximum fundamental stage, the universe operates like a pc, processing facts via discrete units, similar to how a digital laptop uses binary code to system records. According to this view, the physical universe can be defined in phrases of records processing, with area, time, and depend representing distinctive forms of records being processed in line with the laws of physics.

This angle is in particular obtrusive in theories such as quantum computing, which explores how quantum mechanics may want to enable information processing in basically different methods than classical computing. Quantum computing harnesses the peculiar and counterintuitive residences of quantum mechanics, including superposition and entanglement, to technique statistics in parallel, potentially supplying considerable increases in computational power. In this mild, the laws of physics themselves can be visible as a form of quantum computation, in which the evolution of the universe follows quantum-like algorithms that manage records throughout space-time.

The relationship among physical legal guidelines and statistics processing will become in particular clean in the context of thermodynamics, in particular the second regulation of thermodynamics. This regulation, which states that the overall entropy (or sickness) of an remoted system constantly increases through the years, may be interpreted via the lens of statistics idea. Entropy, in this context, is frequently described as a measure of records. In thermodynamics, a machine's entropy will increase when the available facts approximately its country will become greater unpredictable or disordered.

In information theory, entropy quantifies uncertainty or the quantity of facts required to explain a gadget's state. The 2nd law of thermodynamics indicates that as facts is lost or turns into more disordered, the general entropy of the system increases. This connection between entropy and information provides a framework for know-how how physical processes in the universe evolve, not best in phrases of electricity and remember however also as a float of records.

One of the most putting intersections among bodily laws and data concept takes place within the subject of quantum records concept. Quantum mechanics, with its probabilistic nature and ability to explain phenomena like superposition and entanglement, has revolutionized our expertise of data at the quantum stage. In quantum computing, quantum bits (qubits) can exist in more than one states concurrently, bearing in mind a appreciably special shape of facts processing.

Quantum facts idea seeks to recognize how quantum systems keep, procedure, and transmit statistics. One of the vital insights of this field is that quantum facts is concern to physical constraints, such as the no-cloning theorem, which states that quantum information can't be copied exactly. These constraints are at once tied to the laws of quantum mechanics, illustrating how statistics and bodily legal guidelines are interdependent.

Furthermore, the idea of quantum entanglement—a phenomenon in which the kingdom of 1 particle is instantly related to the state of some other, regardless of the space among them—indicates that statistics is not localized however is rather shared across the entire quantum gadget. This interconnectedness is a essential element of the universe's informational structure, and it may have implications for knowledge the nature of area, time, and causality.

A particularly thrilling development within the intersection of physics and data idea is the concept that space-time itself can be an emergent phenomenon springing up from underlying informational tactics. The holographic principle, proposed via physicists like Leonard Susskind and Gerard 't Hooft, shows that the 3-dimensional universe we study may be encoded on a two-dimensional surface at the occasion horizon of a black hollow. In this view, records about the universe isn't always saved inside the traditional feel however is encoded inside the fluctuations of area-time itself.

This concept is intently related to the idea of quantum gravity, which seeks to reconcile widespread relativity (the theory of gravity) with quantum mechanics. In the holographic model, space-time is not fundamental, however as a substitute, it emerges from the data contained on a decrease-dimensional floor. This suggests that the essential structure of the universe may be informational at its core, and the bodily laws we observe are sincerely the policies governing the flow and processing of this statistics.

In addition to explaining the conduct of particles and fields, facts processing also can provide insights into the

Mind and Simulation

evolution of complicated systems. The laws of physics govern now not most effective the movement of fundamental debris but additionally the formation of complex systems, from galaxies to organic organisms. The upward push of complexity within the universe may be understood as the end result of records processing over time.

One instance of that is the evolution of lifestyles, which can be visible as a method of facts processing in a biological machine. The genetic code, saved in DNA, is a form of records that encodes the commands for constructing and keeping dwelling organisms. The rules of evolution, as described via Darwinian principle, can be understood as algorithms that procedure facts approximately environmental conditions and genetic variant, leading to the variation of organisms to their surroundings.

Similarly, the rise of intelligence and focus can be interpreted as a more advanced shape of records processing. The human mind, with its network of neurons and synapses, techniques great quantities of information from the surroundings, permitting us to perceive, suppose, and act in response to the world round us. The thoughts, on this view, is an records processor that interacts with the bodily world, influencing and being prompted by using the legal guidelines of physics.

Fevzi H.

The courting between physical laws and information processing factors to a deeper, extra essential connection among the workings of the universe and the nature of records. As we discover the universe via the lens of records idea, we start to see the possibility that the cosmos itself can be a giant computational device, where bodily laws are the algorithms that govern the drift of statistics. Whether we're reading the behavior of particles, the evolution of existence, or the nature of space-time, we discover that statistics processing is at the heart of the universe's shape and evolution. The legal guidelines of physics are not merely descriptions of the arena around us—they may be the guidelines that dictate how facts is processed, transformed, and transmitted at some stage in the cosmos. As our information of both physics and facts principle deepens, we may also come to see the universe as now not best a place of count number and power however as a massive, interconnected system of records in movement.

5.3 Fractal Structures in the Universe and Algorithmic Reality

The idea of fractals, which describe self-replicating, geometrically complex styles determined in nature, has spread out exciting discussions in each mathematics and cosmology. These tricky structures, determined in the whole thing from snowflakes to galaxies, factor to a hidden order that underlies the apparently chaotic structures of our universe. Fractals, characterised by using their self-similarity at every scale, offer a completely unique lens via which we will discover the universe's structure, revealing a deep connection among geometry, herbal patterns, and the laws of physics.

Fractals are regularly defined as shapes or systems that exhibit self-similarity, which means they repeat the same patterns at special scales. The mathematician Benoît B. Mandelbrot popularized this concept in the overdue twentieth century, especially with the Mandelbrot set, which visually demonstrates the limitless complexity of fractals. The placing characteristic of fractals is that their certain shape remains the same, no matter how tons they are magnified. For instance, a coastline may additionally appear jagged from a distance, but upon nearer inspection, it famous the same irregularity on smaller scales. This self-comparable property is what sets fractals aside from conventional geometric shapes, which might be often easy and predictable.

Mathematically, fractals are frequently defined using recursive algorithms, where a easy rule is repeatedly carried out to generate a complex sample. These patterns may be defined with the aid of particular equations that give rise to systems with limitless complexity notwithstanding being generated by using simple iterative steps. Fractals aren't just a interest of mathematical idea—they're essential to information natural phenomena, from the branching of timber to the formation of mountains, clouds, or even the distribution of galaxies within the cosmos.

Fractal systems are gift at diverse scales during the universe. On the cosmic scale, we have a look at the formation of galaxy clusters that showcase fractal-like patterns. Galaxies are not dispensed lightly throughout the universe; alternatively, they shape complicated, filamentary systems that resemble the self-similar houses of fractals. This cosmic web, additionally called the "cosmic filaments," indicates that the huge-scale shape of the universe might be inherently fractal, with galaxies and clusters organized in a repeating, hierarchical pattern.

The distribution of matter within the universe follows a fractal-like pattern, with voids (sizable empty areas) interspersed with huge clusters of galaxies, all forming a shape that mirrors the self-similar nature of fractals. These systems are notion to emerge from the complex interactions of gravity, dark rely, and the initial conditions set at some stage in the early stages of the universe's formation. The manner those large-scale styles repeat at smaller scales—just as fractals do—indicates that there is an underlying algorithm that governs the universe's structure.

On a extra granular degree, fractal patterns seem in the formation of celestial bodies, which include planets, stars, or even the difficult shape of nebulae. The dirt clouds from which stars shape often show self-similar, fractal-like shapes, while the accretion disks of black holes additionally demonstrate comparable capabilities. These patterns aren't simply aesthetic curiosities; they mirror deep, underlying bodily approaches that are likely governed by way of the legal guidelines of physics themselves.

Fractal systems aren't restricted to the cosmos. In nature, fractals may be found in the whole thing from the branches of timber to the vascular systems in animals and the branching of rivers. These patterns are noticeably green in nature, bearing in mind best distribution of assets across various systems. For instance, the branching of timber and plants is optimized for maximizing publicity to sunlight whilst minimizing the strength required for boom. Similarly, the shape of the human circulatory system, with its branching veins and arteries, follows a fractal sample that optimizes the delivery of oxygen and nutrients for the duration of the body.

The presence of fractals in biological systems has caused good sized insights into how complex systems evolve to maximize efficiency and reduce entropy. The recursive approaches visible in these patterns are a testament to the performance of herbal algorithms, which are fashioned by way of evolutionary pressures. These algorithms aren't explicitly designed, but they emerge naturally because the maximum efficient way to clear up issues associated with area, sources, and electricity distribution.

The complex patterns observed in dwelling organisms replicate an optimization method that arises from the herbal laws of physics, arithmetic, and biology. Evolution has preferred these self-replicating algorithms because they lead to greater resilient, green, and adaptive organisms. In this manner, fractals are each a mathematical curiosity and a powerful tool in understanding the deep tactics that govern life itself.

The concept that the universe might perform consistent with algorithmic policies is a profound one that intersects with concepts from pc technology, records idea, and quantum mechanics. If we view the universe as a large computational system, the fundamental physical procedures might be visible as algorithms that encode the evolution of the universe. Just as fractals emerge from easy recursive guidelines, the giant complexity of the universe may want to rise up from essential algorithms that govern the whole thing from particle interactions to cosmic formations.

This belief has been explored in various approaches, in particular inside the field of virtual physics, which posits that the universe is, in a few feel, a computational entity. According to this view, space, time, and count won't be non-stop but alternatively discrete, made of the smallest gadgets of statistics, just like pixels on a display screen or bits in a laptop software.

The legal guidelines of physics would then be seen because the computational rules that manual the interaction and transformation of those fundamental gadgets of records.

Fractals, on this context, are a reflection of the algorithmic nature of the universe. The self-replicating patterns we study in nature and the cosmos can be the result of underlying algorithms at play on more than one scales. Just as laptop algorithms are used to generate complicated visible patterns from simple regulations, the laws of physics might be understood as algorithms that generate the complex and numerous structures located inside the universe.

One of the most interesting implications of fractal geometry in terms of the universe's shape comes from the holographic precept, which suggests that the universe might be basically -dimensional however appears 3-dimensional to us. According to this principle, all the data contained inside a extent of area can be encoded on its boundary, similar to a hologram. This radical idea challenges our information of area and time, suggesting that the 3-dimensional truth we experience is probably an emergent property of deeper, underlying structures.

In the context of fractals, the holographic principle indicates that the apparently infinite complexity of the universe will be encoded in a less difficult, underlying pattern. The self-comparable properties of fractals align with the holographic

Fevzi H.

view of the universe, in which each a part of the universe contains statistics approximately the entire. This idea should give an explanation for why fractal-like structures seem in each the large-scale cosmic web and the microscopic details of quantum mechanics. The universe may, in truth, be a holographic fractal, in which each a part of the universe reflects the entire, simply as every generation of a fractal reflects the pattern of the bigger shape.

Quantum mechanics, with its peculiar and counterintuitive standards, additionally gives insights into the connection among fractals and the fabric of fact. At the quantum level, the behavior of debris appears to be ruled by probabilistic patterns rather than deterministic laws. These probabilistic distributions frequently show off fractal-like homes, in which the results of quantum occasions aren't completely predictable but display styles that repeat at various scales.

The concept of fractals can help give an explanation for phenomena inclusive of quantum tunneling, where particles seem to skip thru barriers they ought to not be capable of cross. This phenomenon, which defies classical physics, might be understood as a manifestation of the algorithmic, fractal nature of quantum mechanics. Just as fractals showcase complexity that emerges from simple recursive rules, quantum events will be the result of underlying probabilistic algorithms that govern the conduct of debris in a non-linear style.

Fractals provide a window into expertise the complex and deeply ordered nature of the universe. Whether we're looking at the formation of galaxies, the structure of living organisms, or the conduct of quantum debris, fractals seem as a ordinary theme. This self-comparable, recursive nature points to an underlying computational technique—a fixed of algorithms that shape the evolution of the universe at all ranges. The idea that the universe may be a fractal, ruled with the aid of algorithmic guidelines, is a profound one which challenges our traditional notions of area, time, and reality itself. As we retain to discover the intersection of arithmetic, physics, and statistics theory, the idea of a fractal universe may offer critical insights into the private mysteries of life.

5.4 Information on the Planck Scale: Evidence for the Universe's Digital Nature

The Planck scale, which refers to the smallest possible devices of space and time, is one of the most charming and mysterious domain names of theoretical physics. At this scale, the results of quantum gravity come to be big, and the easy continuum of space and time, as defined with the aid of classical physics, breaks down into discrete units. It is at this scale that the possibility arises that the universe can be fundamentally digital, consisting of discrete, quantized units of records instead of a non-stop space-time continuum.

At the Planck scale, the fabric of area-time is predicted to be pretty granular, composed of the smallest feasible devices of duration and time. This concept demanding situations our classical expertise of area-time as a continuous entity. In classical physics, area and time are handled as easy, non-stop backgrounds inside which physical activities occur. However, whilst thinking about the intense conditions close to the Planck scale, the smoothness of area-time may also damage down, leading to a discrete shape governed by means of quantum gravity.

Theoretical fashions, together with loop quantum gravity and string theory, advocate that space-time isn't always non-stop on the smallest scales however alternatively composed of discrete units, comparable to pixels on a display. These fashions suggest that the geometry of space-time turns into quantized at the Planck scale, with each unit representing the smallest viable "bite" of area. Just as digital snap shots are composed of discrete pixels that collectively shape a non-stop photo, the universe can be made of discrete bits of facts that, while mixed, appear non-stop to large scales.

Quantum data concept, which offers with the processing and transmission of quantum data, offers a compelling framework for knowledge the feasible virtual nature of the universe. Quantum bits, or qubits, are the fundamental units of quantum information, analogous to classical bits in conventional computing. However, unlike classical bits, that are either 0 or 1, qubits can exist in superposition, representing more than one states simultaneously. This allows quantum computers to carry out complex calculations that classical computers cannot achieve in reasonable time.

The principles of quantum data theory advocate that the universe can be fundamentally composed of information at its middle. In this view, the universe is not a continuous entity however instead a massive computational system that methods statistics on the quantum stage. Each quantum kingdom may be notion of as a "bit" of records, and the evolution of the universe can be visible as the processing of those bits according to the rules of quantum mechanics. In this digital conception of truth, area-time and count number aren't unbiased entities but are as a substitute manifestations of underlying quantum information.

This attitude has profound implications for our understanding of the universe. If the universe is fundamentally virtual, then the legal guidelines of physics themselves can be the outcomes of algorithms that manage and system data. Just as a computer application generates complicated behaviors from simple instructions, the universe may be the made from

Fevzi H.

an difficult set of computational rules that govern the interactions of quantum bits.

The holographic principle is a theoretical concept in physics that suggests that all the information contained inside a location of area can be encoded at the boundary of that vicinity. This radical concept, which emerged from considerations of black holes and quantum gravity, implies that the three-dimensional universe we perceive might be an emergent property of -dimensional statistics encoded on a distant boundary. In this view, area-time and the items within it are not essential however are as an alternative the result of deeper, informational structures.

The holographic precept has led a few physicists to recommend that the universe itself can be a sort of "hologram" created via the processing of quantum facts. This idea aligns with the belief of a virtual universe, where the continuous enjoy of space and time arises from the manipulation of discrete information. If the universe is indeed holographic and facts is encoded on boundaries, this will advocate that reality itself is essentially virtual, with the smooth, continuous revel in of the universe springing up from discrete, quantized gadgets of facts.

Black holes, that are areas of area in which gravity is so robust that now not even light can get away, provide some other intriguing street for exploring the virtual nature of the universe. The facts paradox related to black holes—the query of what happens to the statistics that falls into a black hole—has led to tremendous tendencies within the know-how of data principle and quantum mechanics. According to classical physics, any information that enters a black hole is lost, main to the so-called "information loss paradox." However, latest developments in quantum gravity and string principle advise that facts is not misplaced but is instead encoded on the occasion horizon of the black hollow, the boundary beyond which not anything can get away.

This concept is consistent with the idea of a digital universe, where records is encoded in discrete bits at the event horizon. Some researchers advocate that the occasion horizon of a black hole may additionally function as a "pixelated" boundary, where the statistics contained inside the black hollow is encoded as discrete gadgets, much like the way digital pics are composed of pixels. This implies that the very fabric of space-time, even in severe conditions like the ones near black holes, can be inherently virtual, with the non-stop glide of data governed with the aid of discrete devices.

The lifestyles of Planck gadgets, which define the smallest feasible values for space, time, and electricity, in addition supports the concept that the universe is digital in nature. These fundamental devices of size, beyond which classical physics breaks down, are regular with the idea of a "digital" universe wherein truth consists of discrete bits of data.

The quantization of energy and area at the Planck scale may be seen as proof that the universe is basically a computational system running on a quantum degree.

The speculation that the universe is virtual in nature is further supported through the idea of simulations. Some researchers have proposed that our truth is probably a simulation run via a complicated civilization. This "simulation speculation" indicates that the universe is not a physical entity but a complicated computer program jogging on a few superior computational system. In this view, the essential debris of depend, the legal guidelines of physics, and even the material of space-time itself will be the result of computational methods.

The concept that the universe is a simulation is steady with the digital nature of fact, where space-time is made up of discrete bits of records. If the universe have been indeed a simulation, it'd suggest that the information encoded within the simulation follows a set of computational policies that govern the behavior of the entirety within the simulated environment. This view aligns with the growing proof from quantum records concept and the holographic precept, both of which advocate that information, in preference to count number, is the most essential building block of truth.

The evidence pointing toward a digital universe turns into more compelling while we bear in mind the intense situations of the Planck scale. At this scale, space-time appears to be discrete, governed by using the regulations of quantum facts principle and quantum gravity. Whether thru the quantization of space-time, the holographic precept, or the behavior of black holes, the concept that the universe is basically digital gains further support. As we preserve to explore the character of reality via quantum mechanics, facts theory, and the study of black holes, it turns into increasingly clean that the universe might not be a non-stop, analog entity but a substantial, complicated virtual machine, with area, time, and rely all emerging from the processing of fundamental quantum bits of information.

5.5 *Quantum Computers and Reality Simulation*

Quantum computer systems represent a groundbreaking advancement in computational electricity, harnessing the unusual residences of quantum mechanics to carry out calculations a ways past the functionality of classical computer systems. As quantum computing generation progresses, the concept that those machines can be used to simulate truth itself has come to be a topic of good sized hobby. Quantum computer systems have the capacity now not only to revolutionize fields together with cryptography, artificial intelligence, and material technological know-how but also to provide us with equipment to simulate complex systems, doubtlessly even the cloth of the universe. The intersection of quantum computing and the concept of truth simulation raises profound questions about the character of life, data, and the boundaries of what is feasible in the digital realm.

Quantum mechanics, the department of physics that deals with the behavior of particles on the atomic and subatomic stages, introduces concepts that defy classical good judgment. Key amongst these is superposition, in which particles can exist in multiple states concurrently, and entanglement, wherein debris can be immediately linked, no matter distance. These properties provide quantum computers with a unique gain: even as classical bits can represent most effective one in every of two states (0 or 1) at any given time, quantum bits (qubits) can represent both zero and 1 at once, way to superposition. This capacity allows quantum computers to carry out many calculations simultaneously, exponentially growing their computational strength.

The potential of quantum computing lies now not simply in the pace of calculations, but in the types of problems it may solve. Certain troubles that could take classical computer systems millennia to resolve will be completed by way of a quantum computer in a fragment of the time. This consists of responsibilities which includes factoring big numbers, optimizing complicated structures, and simulating quantum bodily structures, all of which are primary to the concept of simulating truth.

At its center, a simulation is a model or representation of a real-world device, and the extra complex the device, the extra difficult it becomes to simulate appropriately. Classical computer systems regularly warfare with this, mainly when simulating the behavior of quantum structures, as they require sizable computational assets to version even easy quantum interactions. Quantum computers, but, are inherently applicable to this task. Since they operate the usage of quantum concepts themselves, they can simulate quantum structures with a long way more performance than classical computer systems.

One of the maximum thrilling possibilities for quantum computing is the simulation of physical phenomena at scales and resolutions formerly unimaginable. This includes simulating molecular interactions, the conduct of materials under excessive conditions, and even the properties of fundamental debris in excessive-strength environments. By as it should be simulating those methods, quantum computers ought to result in breakthroughs in a extensive range of fields, along with drug improvement, cloth technology, and electricity production. Moreover, the capability to simulate such structures on a quantum laptop may also make bigger to the introduction of complete virtual universes—simulations of fact that are ruled by means of the equal bodily legal guidelines we examine.

The concept of truth simulation—in which a pc, in particular a quantum laptop, creates a virtual international indistinguishable from the physical international—has been a famous challenge of philosophical hypothesis and scientific inquiry. The idea suggests that truth itself can be the result of a large computational technique, with the universe functioning as a kind of simulation run via some advanced entity or machine. This concept, frequently known as the "simulation hypothesis," has won traction in latest years, in particular with improvements in computing power and our understanding of quantum mechanics.

Quantum computers ought to offer the way to simulate truth at an unheard of stage of detail. Unlike classical simulations, that are constrained with the aid of the need to approximate continuous variables, quantum simulations ought to model the continuous nature of space-time and quantum procedures precisely, with out lack of fidelity. If quantum computers are able to simulating the universe with this degree of precision, it raises the interesting possibility that reality itself will be a simulation—possibly even one this is deliberately designed and maintained with the aid of an advanced civilization or a few different external pressure.

Mind and Simulation

To simulate fact on a quantum computer, one would want to model not just person quantum structures, but the complete structure of the universe, together with area-time, gravity, and the fundamental laws of physics. This is a enormous project, however quantum computer systems have the ability to perform this sort of simulation due to the fact they operate using the very same ideas that govern the conduct of the universe. By encoding the legal guidelines of physics into the computation itself, a quantum computer ought to simulate everything from the interactions of subatomic particles to the dynamics of galaxies, potentially reproducing the complete observable universe at the quantum level.

One of the key additives of simulating truth on a quantum pc is the need to model quantum entanglement and the interconnectedness of all debris. In a quantum simulation of reality, every particle could be entangled with others, and the state of the whole machine would need to be updated concurrently throughout all scales of life. This is far beyond the capabilities of classical computing, but quantum computer systems are designed to handle such interconnected systems due to their inherent capability to symbolize a couple of states right away and system information in parallel.

While the potential for quantum computer systems to simulate truth is exciting, there are numerous challenges and limitations that need to be addressed. One of the number one boundaries is the problem of scalability. Quantum computer systems, as they exist nowadays, are still of their infancy. Current quantum processors are fairly small, with only a few dozen qubits, which limits their capability to carry out huge-scale simulations. In order to simulate even a small portion of the universe, quantum computers might need to scale up to thousands or thousands and thousands of qubits, requiring advances in quantum error correction, hardware stability, and qubit coherence.

Moreover, there are fundamental questions about the character of truth itself that should be addressed earlier than we will fully simulate it. For instance, quantum mechanics suggests that the very act of statement impacts the machine being observed, a phenomenon called the observer effect. This poses a task for simulating a fact this is goal and independent of the observer. If the universe itself is a simulation, how would we reconcile the observer impact with the idea of an outside "fact"?

Additionally, simulating the entire universe at a quantum degree can be impractical because of the monstrous computational sources required. While quantum computer systems can simulate unique quantum structures with high-quality performance, modeling a whole universe—complete with all its interactions and complexities—could require an astronomical amount of processing energy. As a end result, even quantum computers may face obstacles in their capability to simulate fact with complete accuracy.

The concept that quantum computers ought to simulate entire realities raises profound ethical and philosophical questions. If it have been possible to simulate a really perfect replica of the universe, or even a aware being inside a simulation, what implications might this have for our information of lifestyles? Could we be residing in any such simulation right now? If we were to create simulated worlds with aware entities, would the ones entities have rights, and the way might we deal with them?

Furthermore, the ability to simulate truth may want to have a long way-reaching consequences within the realms of artificial intelligence, virtual truth, and human focus. If we are able to simulate the legal guidelines of physics and recreate the universe's complexity, should we also simulate human attention? Would it be viable to add a human thoughts right into a quantum simulation, essentially developing virtual immortality? These questions push the boundaries of what it way to be human and venture our knowledge of life, identification, and truth itself.

Quantum computers maintain the ability to revolutionize our capability to simulate complex structures, along with the very nature of fact itself. While we're nevertheless within the early levels of growing quantum computing generation, the

Fevzi H.

opportunities for future applications—mainly in the field of reality simulation—are giant. As quantum computers evolve, they will provide us with the gear to no longer handiest understand the universe at a deeper stage however additionally to recreate it in virtual shape. However, as we undertaking into this new frontier, it is important to don't forget the moral and philosophical implications of such generation, as it challenges the very foundations of what we perceive as truth. The destiny of quantum simulation, while nevertheless uncertain, promises to reshape our knowledge of existence, the universe, and our place within it.

CHAPTER 6

Physical Simulations and Virtual Realities

6.1 Simulating the Universe with Modern Computers

Technological advancements and the increasing power of computers have made the concept of creating a simulation of the physical universe more sensible. Today, pc technological know-how and physics, especially inside the simulation of complicated structures, have made extensive development.

A simulation is a system used to create a version of the real global. Typically, this process is controlled by means of mathematical modeling, computer software program, and hardware. Simulations intention to imitate the physical events and behaviors of the real world. Today, it's miles feasible to simulate the physical universe at each the micro and macro ranges. These simulations can be carried out at numerous scales, from atomic-stage debris to the movements of galaxies.

Simulations of the physical universe preserve big fee in fields like cosmology, astrophysics, and particle physics. They allow researchers to recognize how all interactions in the universe comply with physical legal guidelines. For instance, astrophysicists use complex algorithms to simulate the formation of galaxies, at the same time as particle physicists practice a similar technique to version interactions on the subatomic level.

These simulations assist us realize the most fundamental functions of the universe. For instance, modeling phenomena related to black holes and darkish count, that are too remote or mysterious to be determined at once, permits for a better expertise. Scientists can have a look at how physical laws feature via simulations, leading to the development of theories approximately how the universe works.

Simulating the universe requires full-size computing electricity. Today, computer systems are able to processing hundreds of thousands, even billions, of statistics factors simultaneously. This capability enables the simulation of various stages of the bodily global. High-decision supercomputers provide the computational energy necessary for simulating physical events.

For instance, simulating on the "Planck Scale" entails interactions which are noticeably complicated, and traditional computers cannot version them. However, improvements in quantum computers and parallel processing networks make these types of simulations feasible. These computers can process good sized information sets a good deal faster and greater efficiently, enabling the correct modeling of severa interactions within the bodily world.

These computer systems can also carry out simulations based totally on records received from particle accelerators. In those experiments, simulations recreate subatomic-stage bodily events, which aren't possible to take a look at without delay. This allows physicists to model interactions at a microscopic scale, leading to deeper insights into fundamental physics.

Simulations are useful not handiest on the microscopic level however also at the macroscopic scale. Cosmological simulations are one of the maximum significant equipment in understanding the nature of the universe. Many astrophysicists use supercomputers to simulate the formation of galaxies, stars, and even the complete universe. These simulations permit us to model the procedures and evolution of the universe from its early levels.

For instance, projects simulating the "Big Bang" model have made considerable progress in expertise the situations that existed at the beginning of the universe. These simulations display how huge-scale systems along with galaxy clusters, stars, and black holes fashioned. They additionally assist researchers understand the behavior of darkish rely and dark power—additives of the universe that cannot be immediately found however constitute a massive part of its mass.

Simulations like these model how the merging and collision of galaxies arise, or how new systems form when galaxies interact. They additionally simulate how gasoline behaves around black holes and the way galaxies evolve. These insights assist build a clearer picture of the universe's dynamic methods.

The destiny of simulations is carefully tied to technologies like synthetic intelligence (AI) and deep gaining knowledge of. These technology should permit for even more specific and accurate simulations of the universe. AI can automate the modeling of complicated bodily processes, growing the performance of simulations. Deep getting to know algorithms could speed up simulations and allow for the processing of even large data sets.

Additionally, AI and deep learning techniques can enhance the analysis of records obtained from simulations. This will play an important position in growing new cosmological fashions and bodily theories. Deep gaining knowledge of can examine from the consequences of simulations and are expecting destiny physical activities with greater accuracy.

In the destiny, simulations will not only model physical activities but additionally offer new views on the unknown aspects of the universe. These technologies will allow deeper knowledge of the physical world at a good deal finer tiers.

Simulating the universe the use of cutting-edge computers performs a important role in supporting us apprehend the structure of the universe, but it also increases profound questions about the nature of reality itself. If we can correctly version the universe via simulation, it shows that the whole lot we understand as fact is probably open to thinking.

Fevzi H.

Seeing how bodily legal guidelines and mathematical formulas paintings as it should be via a simulation provides a unique possibility to recognize the essential workings of the universe.

The development of simulations is big not only for scientific research but also for those in search of solutions to philosophical questions. The nature of truth may be extra genuinely understood thru simulations, tough our perceptions and assumptions about life. These improvements are reshaping the limits between technological know-how, philosophy, and era, and they're deepening our know-how of the way the universe functions.

6.2 Artificial Intelligence-Powered Virtual Realities

The development of artificial intelligence (AI) has end up a pivotal detail in creating an increasing number of sophisticated virtual realities. Virtual realities, as soon as limited to the world of entertainment and gaming, have advanced into complex, interactive environments powered with the aid of AI. These AI-driven virtual worlds are now used in fields starting from schooling and education to simulation, leisure, or even social interaction.

At its middle, an AI-powered virtual truth is a simulated environment where the dynamics and interactions in the world are driven and influenced via AI. Unlike conventional video

video games or computer-generated environments that comply with predefined scripts and actions, AI-stronger virtual realities are designed to evolve and evolve based on the conduct and choices of the customers inside them. This allows for a more dynamic, responsive, and personalised experience.

These virtual environments commonly consist of immersive, three-dimensional worlds wherein customers can have interaction with different users, digital characters, and the surroundings itself. The intelligence embedded in these worlds makes the interactions experience extra natural, realistic, and engaging, regularly blurring the line between the actual and virtual worlds.

AI performs a essential role in constructing digital realities that are not static, but instead, interactive and responsive. Traditionally, virtual worlds have been constrained to pre-programmed moves, with interactions and activities unfolding according to set styles. However, the mixing of AI has added approximately a transformative shift in how virtual environments reply to users.

AI algorithms, including device mastering and natural language processing, permit virtual characters or retailers to respond dynamically to user enter. These sellers can recognize context, study from user interactions, and adapt over time. For example, an AI-pushed individual in a digital international might recognize a person's behavior patterns, emotional tone, or specific preferences, and alter its responses consequently. This allows for personalised interactions that evolve as the user engages greater with the surroundings.

In more advanced eventualities, AI systems inside those virtual worlds can expect person moves and create environments that adapt in actual-time. For instance, if a consumer expresses interest in exploring certain varieties of landscapes or sports, the digital international ought to dynamically adjust its functions to provide new content material that aligns with the ones options.

One of the maximum good sized advances in AI-powered virtual realities is the evolution of non-player characters (NPCs). These characters, who had been as soon as limited to easy roles, now showcase more complex behaviors and interactions, way to AI. NPCs, traditionally controlled by recreation common sense, can now interact in sensible conversations, don't forget beyond interactions, and respond to the person in nuanced and practical methods.

With AI, NPCs are not sure by using scripted dialogue timber or fixed patterns of conduct. Instead, they can use herbal language processing (NLP) to understand and reply to consumer speech, developing a greater fluid and natural interplay. These NPCs would possibly even simulate emotions, explicit their thoughts, and form dynamic relationships with customers, including depth to virtual worlds.

For example, in digital education simulations, AI-powered NPCs can act as digital instructors, education users thru scenarios, presenting remarks, and adapting the problem level based on the consumer's overall performance. In entertainment, NPCs can enhance the storyline with the aid of reacting to a participant's selections, making every experience sense precise and unpredictable.

AI doesn't just enhance the characters inside digital environments; it also shapes the environments themselves. AI-powered systems can create procedurally generated worlds, which are dynamically designed and altered primarily based on the actions and behaviors of the person. These environments aren't static, however as an alternative adapt in real-time, presenting a honestly immersive experience.

For example, AI can generate landscapes that evolve through the years based on consumer interplay, or simulate ecosystems wherein flowers, animals, and weather styles exchange in response to outside factors. This degree of complexity makes virtual worlds sense alive and reactive to the consumer's movements, main to a heightened feel of immersion.

Moreover, AI also can be used to create sensible systems that control the virtual world, making sure that the world's inner common sense remains coherent. Whether it's simulating the physics of a digital surroundings, coping with complicated social systems, or maintaining the realism of interactions between virtual entities, AI is the backbone that guarantees these digital environments operate easily.

While AI-powered virtual realities provide enormous possibilities, additionally they raise vital moral questions. One of the most vast worries revolves around the blurring of the line between reality and simulation. As these virtual environments turn out to be extra sophisticated and indistinguishable from real existence, customers may additionally revel in an increasing experience of attachment to those simulated worlds. This may want to have profound mental consequences, especially if customers begin to decide upon the digital world over the real one.

Additionally, the rapid development of AI in digital realities could increase concerns about privacy, records protection, and control. Since AI systems in those virtual worlds are capable of accumulating huge quantities of facts about customers' behaviors, choices, and interactions, there are ability dangers concerning the misuse or exploitation of this facts.

Furthermore, there is the issue of addiction to virtual worlds. With AI-pushed environments turning into greater fascinating, customers may additionally locate themselves spending growing amounts of time in those simulations. This could result in a detachment from fact, as individuals lose interest in actual-global reports in prefer of extra idealized or controlled digital ones.

Another key attention is the potential for AI structures to expand beyond human manipulate. As AI grows more advanced, there may be a possibility that it can begin to act in methods that had been now not at the start supposed by its creators. In virtual worlds, this can suggest the emergence of surprising behaviors, where AI entities now not adhere to pre-programmed roles and start to showcase unbiased decision-making methods.

Looking closer to the future, AI's position in virtual realities will possibly hold to make bigger. We can anticipate the improvement of even greater state-of-the-art simulations that leverage advanced AI strategies along with deep learning, reinforcement getting to know, and unsupervised gaining knowledge of. These improvements will allow for even extra realistic and interactive virtual worlds, wherein AI can manage complicated social systems, simulate human behavior more convincingly, and create entirely new styles of enjoyment and interaction.

AI-powered virtual worlds can also have giant packages in areas together with healthcare, schooling, and social integration. Virtual realities will be used to educate medical specialists, provide remedy, or offer digital spaces in which human beings can have interaction in social sports notwithstanding bodily boundaries. These opportunities open the door to a destiny where AI-pushed digital environments are an necessary a part of every day life.

Moreover, as AI technologies hold to enhance, the advent of absolutely immersive and indistinguishable digital realities may also emerge as a reality. With improvements in neural interfaces and brain-computer interactions, users may want to have interaction with these virtual worlds in approaches that have been formerly notion to be not possible, creating a new era of human-computer interaction.

AI-powered virtual realities are pushing the bounds of what we remember feasible in the realm of virtual simulation. They are remodeling how we have interaction with digital worlds, providing new possibilities for enjoyment, socialization, education, and even personal increase. However, they also enhance vital moral and psychological concerns that have to be addressed as these technologies keep to evolve. As AI continues to form the improvement of digital environments, it's going to surely redefine the character of fact itself, tough our perceptions of what's real and what is virtual.

6.3 The Digital Transfer of the Brain and Nervous System

The idea of transferring the mind and nervous machine right into a virtual environment represents one of the most profound and speculative regions of medical exploration. This concept, often called mind uploading or mind-laptop interfacing, involves creating a digital replica of the human mind and its functions, efficaciously moving focus, memories, thoughts, and sensations right into a virtual or digital realm. While this concept may also sound like science fiction, extensive development in neuroscience, synthetic intelligence, and computational modeling is steadily bringing this idea toward reality.

Before exploring how the brain and anxious device can be digitized, it's far essential to understand the complexity of the human brain itself. The brain consists of about 86 billion neurons, each interconnected by way of trillions of synapses. These neurons speak via electric impulses and biochemical alerts, forming a community that is answerable for all cognitive capabilities, consisting of perception, notion, memory, and emotion. The mind's shape and interest are noticeably complicated, and mapping this significant network is a enormous undertaking.

The first step in shifting the brain to a virtual environment entails mapping the complex details of the neural network. This process, frequently referred to as connectomics, pursuits to create a complete map of the connections between neurons, in addition to the styles of their electrical hobby. Techniques along with purposeful magnetic resonance imaging

Fevzi H.

(fMRI), electroencephalography (EEG), and superior neuroimaging strategies are being used to higher recognize brain hobby and connectivity. However, those technology are still within the early levels of imparting the level of detail needed to completely reflect the mind's capability in a digital medium.

One of the primary technologies enabling the virtual transfer of mind pastime is brain-laptop interface (BCI) structures. BCIs allow for direct communique among the mind and external gadgets, bypassing conventional input methods like keyboards or speech. These interfaces are normally finished thru the placement of electrodes at the scalp or via invasive neural implants. BCIs are already being utilized in programs which includes prosthetic manage, communique for individuals with paralysis, or even video game interplay.

However, to upload the whole lot of the mind's hobby right into a virtual form, tons extra sophisticated and effective BCIs are required. These interfaces need to be capable of not just studying mind signals, but also writing records again into the brain. This gives numerous challenges, each from a technical and moral perspective. First, the current resolution of non-invasive methods for monitoring mind pastime is inadequate for shooting the high degree of element required for a virtual duplicate. Invasive techniques, which include implanting electrodes at once into the mind, pose risks including tissue harm, contamination, and the want for lengthy-time period renovation.

Furthermore, the complexity of the mind's approaches means that honestly monitoring neural activity isn't always enough. The digital gadget must additionally simulate the difficult biochemical and electrical signals that arise in the brain, and reproduce them in a way that continues the integrity of cognizance, reminiscence, and identification. Achieving this stage of precision and constancy is a formidable assignment, one that can require breakthroughs in both neuroscience and technology.

Once we are able to map the brain and interface with its neural strategies, the following step is growing a version or simulation of the mind's capabilities. The intention is to broaden an artificial gadget which could reflect the mind's shape and conduct, not simply in a mechanical experience but in a conscious, sentient manner.

Supercomputers, artificial intelligence, and gadget studying algorithms will play key roles in simulating mind hobby. The most superior fashions of the brain will possibly use neural networks, a type of AI designed to imitate the structure and operation of biological neural networks. These networks can be skilled to process facts in approaches much like how the mind does, probably bearing in mind the introduction of virtual minds that showcase comparable developments to human cognizance.

However, simulating a human brain is a very resource-extensive method. The human brain's hobby generates an enormous amount of facts, and replicating its complexity on a digital platform will require huge computational energy and reminiscence. To date, efforts to simulate complete brains have been restricted to less complicated organisms, along with the nematode C. Elegans, which contains handiest 302 neurons. The human brain, with its billions of neurons and trillions of synaptic connections, gives an entirely extraordinary scale of complexity.

As computational strength advances, we may additionally see greater formidable attempts to simulate human-stage cognition. Projects just like the Human Brain Project in Europe and the Brain Initiative inside the United States are aiming to create complete mind models, although these initiatives are nevertheless of their infancy as compared to the size required for full mind transfer.

The idea of digitizing the brain and importing attention right into a machine raises profound ethical and philosophical questions. At the core of this difficulty is the character of attention and identification. If the mind is efficiently replicated in a virtual surroundings, is the ensuing cognizance truely the same as the original? Or does the virtual model turn out to be a separate entity, despite the fact that it possesses the identical memories, thoughts, and behaviors?

One of the most urgent concerns is the continuity of cognizance. If a person's mind is uploaded to a computer, will they keep the same sense of self, or will they in reality emerge as a duplicate of the original person? This touches on deeper philosophical debates about the nature of the soul, private identification, and the difference between physical and virtual existence.

There are also issues about the potential results of importing minds into virtual spaces. If digital consciousnesses turn out to be a truth, it can cause a new elegance of beings living in a merely virtual global. These beings may experience a extraordinary sort of life, one that is detached from the physical realm. Such a shift could alter the very nature of human existence and raise questions on the rights and freedoms of virtual beings.

Moreover, importing cognizance ought to create electricity imbalances, in which the rich or effective people who can have the funds for mind importing could basically obtain immortality, whilst others are left in the back of in the physical global. This may want to exacerbate existing societal inequalities and create a new shape of digital elitism.

While the virtual switch of the brain may also look like a distant destiny opportunity, its implications are already being felt in positive areas of society. Technologies like BCIs are already getting used to repair lost features in people with neurological problems or spinal cord injuries. These advances have the potential to hugely improve the exceptional of life for people with disabilities.

The capability to upload the brain right into a digital format may want to in addition revolutionize healthcare by using allowing for the upkeep of cognitive functions in individuals suffering from terminal neurological situations, inclusive of Alzheimer's sickness. In the future, someone with a degenerative mind circumstance may want to potentially "upload" their cognizance earlier than their physical mind deteriorates, permitting them to maintain existing in a digital area.

On a societal degree, mind importing may want to redefine standards of life and demise, individuality, and the role of the human frame. It may open up new possibilities for human interplay, along with fully immersive virtual worlds in which consciousness can roam freely, disconnected from the bodily barriers of the body. However, this can also cause societal fragmentation, as humans may pick out to abandon their bodily bodies in want of digital life, resulting in a divide among those who choose to "upload" and people who remain inside the physical international.

The digital switch of the brain and anxious machine represents one of the most formidable dreams in both neuroscience and generation. While we are nevertheless far from attaining full mind uploading, advances in brain-computer interfaces, AI, and brain simulation are step by step making this concept a extra realistic opportunity. As we flow in the direction of this step forward, it's miles important to cope with the moral, philosophical, and societal challenges that accompany it. The potential to digitize human attention may want to redefine the nature of lifestyles itself, changing our know-how of existence, identity, and what it method to be human.

6.4 The Metaverse, Holographic Universes, and the Evolution of Reality Perception

The idea of a Metaverse—an interconnected, virtual universe wherein customers have interaction with every other and the surroundings via virtual avatars—has rapidly advanced from technology fiction into a focal point of technological improvement and philosophical inquiry. Combined with the belief of holographic universes, this concept affords a profound assignment to our conventional information of reality. What occurs whilst our notion of fact is shaped completely through virtual areas, and how does this shift the bounds among the physical and virtual worlds?

The Metaverse is envisioned as a fully immersive, 3-D virtual environment, frequently defined as the subsequent iteration of the net. Unlike present day internet, that's predominantly a platform for statistics and communication, the Metaverse is designed to be a space where humans can live, work, socialize, and play in actual-time, the usage of virtual avatars to represent themselves. It is an surroundings in which bodily and digital realities are intertwined, with customers experiencing a feel of presence, interaction, and business enterprise as though they were in a bodily global, even though they're interacting via technology.

The Metaverse is made viable via improvements in digital truth (VR), augmented truth (AR), and mixed reality (MR), which permit users to experience virtual environments with a excessive stage of immersion. By carrying headsets or the use of specialized devices, customers can have interaction with holographic projections, virtual gadgets, and different contributors in ways that mimic the sensory revel in of the real global. Platforms like Facebook's Horizon Worlds, Decentraland, and Epic Games' Unreal Engine are building those digital areas, every with its very own layout, motive, and network. Users can explore those worlds, attend events, create virtual goods, and socialize, blurring the lines between the bodily and virtual domains.

This shift in the direction of virtual areas increases key questions about the character of lifestyles and identification. As extra people spend full-size quantities of time within these digital environments, will their sense of self come to be more and more connected to their virtual persona? Could the Metaverse provide a way to transcend the bodily boundaries of the body, making an allowance for more desirable social interplay, innovative expression, or even immortality through the staying power of virtual avatars?

The concept of a holographic universe—suggesting that the universe itself is a projection of data encoded on , - dimensional floor—has emerge as an influential idea in cutting-edge physics. According to the holographic principle, the three-dimensional universe that we experience is a form of "illusion" generated with the aid of the interactions of fundamental particles encoded on a miles lower-dimensional area. This idea, which originated from black hollow thermodynamics and string idea, proposes that every one the information inside the universe is contained inside its boundary, like a hologram.

This concept has profound implications for our knowledge of truth. If the universe is certainly a hologram, then our perception of space, time, and depend can be a projection of facts stored on a distant boundary. This raises

Fevzi H.

questions on the nature of the physical international and the limits of human perception. Could it be that everything we perceive as "actual" is merely a projection—a simulation of kinds—generated via essential data at a stage of truth far past our direct comprehension?

While the holographic precept continues to be a theoretical construct, it has won traction in the subject of theoretical physics as a potential explanation for the paradoxes of quantum mechanics and wellknown relativity. The idea that the complete universe might be a projection has led some to invest approximately the nature of virtual realities and the possibility of making simulated universes with comparable residences. If the physical world is a holographic projection, then growing an synthetic, virtual version of this type of fact—like the Metaverse—will become a greater viable idea, bearing in mind a controlled, programmed universe that mirrors our personal.

The emergence of the Metaverse, alongside theories like the holographic universe, indicates that our perception of truth is becoming more and more malleable. In the virtual age, the bounds between the actual and the digital are blurring, and new varieties of notion are rising. As we engage extra with digital environments, we're redefining what constitutes "real" revel in.

In the past, fact became considered synonymous with the bodily global—what we ought to touch, see, and interact with. But as we increasingly live in a global wherein virtual experiences are just as meaningful as physical ones, this definition is evolving. The Metaverse, particularly, challenges the conventional view of fact by means of offering an environment that feels "real" in terms of emotional and cognitive engagement, although it is totally synthetic. Just as in goals or hallucinations, the brain can revel in a experience of immersion in environments that lack a physical basis.

As human beings spend more time interacting with digital avatars and holographic projections, we might also see a shift in how people relate to their bodily our bodies. The idea of "virtual dualism" indicates that individuals may additionally begin to view their digital selves as distinct entities, leading to a psychological separation among the bodily body and the digital persona. This has the ability to affect self-identification, relationships, and social structures, as people start to navigate a couple of realities concurrently.

One of the maximum good sized results of this shift is the capacity for a reevaluation of the bounds between the digital and bodily worlds. For instance, because the Metaverse grows in sophistication, people may want to experience a feel of possession and organization over their virtual environments. The query then arises: If we are able to create and manipulate complete digital worlds, in which does the distinction among the real and the artificial cease?

Fevzi H.

Holographic era, which tasks 3-dimensional pix into physical area with out the need for glasses or other devices, could in addition blur the strains between the digital and the real. Holograms are already being utilized in enjoyment, advertising and marketing, and medicine, but their capacity extends a long way past those industries. As holographic displays enhance, they will allow us to have interaction with virtual gadgets and environments in approaches that feel increasingly more tangible and sensible.

In the future, holographic generation may want to allow for the advent of completely new kinds of social interplay, training, and enjoyment, wherein human beings can have interaction with digital representations of items, locations, and even other people in actual-time. This has the capacity to redefine how we talk and enjoy the arena, creating an surroundings in which digital and bodily realities coexist in a unbroken, dynamic way.

The mixture of holography, virtual fact, and the Metaverse will in all likelihood lead to an increasing number of sophisticated simulations of the physical global, where distinctions between the two geographical regions end up an increasing number of hard to determine. Such environments ought to foster a new kind of "shared fact," where multiple customers participate in a collective digital enjoy, interacting with every different and with the environment in approaches that mirror the bodily international.

The upward push of virtual environments like the Metaverse and the opportunity of holographic universes boost profound philosophical and moral questions. What does it mean to stay in a virtual global? If we can create a digital truth that feels as real as the physical one, what occurs to the cost of bodily existence? Will humans start to prioritize digital reviews over bodily ones, developing a brand new shape of escapism or maybe a form of immortality within virtual worlds?

Furthermore, if the universe itself is holographic in nature, then the idea of truth might also emerge as an increasing number of summary. What takes place while we recognize that the sector round us can be an illusion, a projection of records encoded on boundary? Does this make the physical international any less "actual," or does it without a doubt redefine our know-how of what fact is?

As virtual and bodily realities maintain to converge, we have to grapple with the consequences for human consciousness, social interaction, and the very nature of lifestyles itself. The future of reality notion is hastily evolving, and the technologies that shape this evolution will fundamentally regulate how we understand and experience the arena round us.

6.5 The Brain, Neuroscience, and the Limits of Simulation Perception

As era advances and the boundary between the actual and the virtual international turns into increasingly difficult to differentiate, the role of the brain and neuroscience in shaping our notion of simulations has come beneath intense scrutiny. The way the mind processes records from its environment, constructs a cohesive experience of self, and responds to sensory stimuli forms the inspiration of our interaction with both the bodily and virtual worlds. Understanding the bounds of simulation perception thru the lens of neuroscience can provide profound insights into the potential—and barriers—of virtual realities, inclusive of digital simulations just like the Metaverse and holographic universes.

At its core, notion is a technique by way of which the mind interprets sensory inputs—whether or not visible, auditory, tactile, or in any other case—and constructs an expertise of the outside global. This manner is a ways from passive; the brain is continuously making predictions and filling in gaps, frequently using previous know-how to interpret incomplete or ambiguous information. This is essential for survival, permitting organisms to make short choices based on confined or imperfect sensory information.

When enticing with simulations, along with virtual environments, the brain techniques digital stimuli in a comparable manner it'd procedure bodily stimuli, the use of the same sensory pathways. However, this technique isn't always faultless, and the brain may be tricked into perceiving digital environments as actual, in particular when those environments are designed to imitate the sensory inputs of the bodily world. This phenomenon has been central to the development of virtual truth (VR), wherein users revel in a heightened feel of immersion and presence in simulated environments.

While VR generation can effectively simulate sensory studies which includes sight and sound, it still falls short in replicating other sensory modalities like contact, flavor, and scent, which stay tough to simulate convincingly. Despite this, the brain is remarkably adept at "filling in the blanks" and can regularly persuade itself that a simulation is real. This highlights the energy of the brain's interpretative mechanisms, however additionally the inherent obstacles when it comes to developing absolutely immersive, multisensory virtual realities.

From a neuroscience attitude, digital and simulated environments aren't fundamentally one-of-a-kind from the bodily international when it comes to how the mind tactics sensory enter. However, there are key differences in how the mind handles the interactions within those spaces. Neuroscientists have shown that after attractive with virtual worlds, the brain can revel in sensory overload or dissonance—in which what we see would not align with other sensory statistics, such as physical sensations. This mismatch, frequently known as sensory conflict, can cause a phenomenon referred to as "motion illness" or "cybersickness" in digital environments, especially whilst there is a disconnect among the movement in a simulation and the shortage of corresponding bodily motion.

Furthermore, the mind's tendency to anticipate that virtual environments are real may have substantial psychological and physiological effects. In situations in which people are deeply immersed in digital worlds—which include inside the Metaverse or through VR gaming—users may additionally revel in changes of their emotional and cognitive states, regularly treating digital reviews as if they have been real. This results in questions on the volume to which simulated environments can have an impact on real-world behavior, feelings, or even identity.

The brain's capability to evolve to and "trust" in simulated environments is likewise constrained with the aid of its need for feedback from the body. For example, whilst interacting with virtual objects or different avatars in VR, the shortage of tactile remarks (the feeling of contact or resistance) frequently disrupts the sense of presence. The mind expects physical comments in the form of proprioception (our sense of body function) and haptic responses (touch sensations), and while these are not gift or are imperfectly simulated, it can purpose the brain to lose confidence inside the realism of the enjoy.

As simulations grow more sophisticated, they may hold to push the bounds of what the brain can understand as actual. However, there are inherent limits to this technique, formed each by the competencies of technology and the character of human perception itself.

One of the fundamental boundaries is the mind's reliance on embodied enjoy. The frame is central to how we interact with the sector, and our sensory organs are deeply incorporated with neural pathways which have advanced to manner the physical world. No rely how convincing a simulation will become, the brain's perception of truth is deeply tied to physical sensations—particularly proprioception and kinesthetic comments. This is why, for instance, VR environments can sense "off" while the person moves around but would not enjoy the corresponding comments of body motion. While there are advances in haptic comments generation that try to address this trouble, it remains a project to recreate the overall range of sensory reviews.

Moreover, there are better-order cognitive techniques, which include emotions, social interaction, and cognizance itself, which may also withstand being completely replicated in a simulation. While digital worlds can mimic social conditions, they can't absolutely replicate the nuance of human emotions,

Fevzi H.

physical presence, and social bonding that are so essential to our revel in of the physical global. For instance, regardless of how sensible a simulated avatar may seem, it could never absolutely capture the emotional weight and subtlety of face-to-face human interplay. In this feel, the "realness" of a digital enjoy is constantly confined through the depth and richness of the sensory and emotional cues which are absent in the digital global.

Another foremost hassle in simulation belief is the incapability to reproduce the complexity of the physical world in all its senses. As we strive to create greater immersive simulations, we are forced to lessen the complexity of physical reality into computable fashions. Whether simulating an environment, a human body, or the universe itself, the sheer quantity of data and variables that have to be encoded in a simulation is superb. The simulation of recognition—if it's miles even viable—calls for a intensity of knowledge that we've yet to completely reap. What makes us human—the very essence of self-recognition and attention—cannot absolutely be decreased to binary code or algorithms, irrespective of how advanced the computational gear grow to be.

As technology progresses, one of the methods that these limits can be mitigated is thru neural interfaces, consisting of mind-computer interfaces (BCIs). These technologies searching for to bridge the gap among the mind and virtual environments, potentially enabling direct communique among the mind and simulations. BCIs have already shown promise in scientific fields, especially for individuals with paralysis, permitting them to manipulate prosthetic limbs and computer cursors the use of their mind.

In the context of digital realities and simulations, BCIs should permit a greater seamless integration among the brain and digital worlds. By at once stimulating the mind's sensory regions, BCIs may want to simulate a broader variety of sensory inputs, including touch, flavor, and even feelings, growing a extra immersive revel in. However, the quantity to which BCIs can enhance or even absolutely reflect the sensory experience of the actual world continues to be in the realm of studies. While the ability exists for those technologies to push the limits of what we understand as real, there continue to be sizeable demanding situations in replicating the complexity of the human enjoy.

Moreover, BCIs may additionally allow for the simulation of cognitive states, which include reminiscence or choice-making methods, which could blur the road among attention and synthetic intelligence. However, moral concerns arise, especially regarding the manipulation of memory, identity, and the ability for changing individuals' perceptions of truth in approaches that would have unexpected results.

Fevzi H.

As simulations grow to be increasingly more advanced and the mind adapts to new virtual realities, the line among the virtual and the actual will keep to blur. However, the limits of human perception and the limitations of neuroscience will continually area boundaries on what can be simulated and the way convincingly those simulations are perceived. The brain's tricky and developed system for interacting with the physical world creates an inherent gap among the sensations and experiences we can simulate digitally and the richness of the actual global.

As we move forward in growing greater immersive simulations, the challenge can be in information those limits and working within them, making sure that virtual realities decorate our lives with out eroding our sense of what is truly actual. The courting between the mind, neuroscience, and the notion of simulations will keep to adapt, because the digital world will become an more and more principal part of our lifestyles.

CHAPTER 7

If We Are in a Simulation, Is Escape Possible?

7.1 Escaping the Simulation: Can We Decode Our Own Code?

The idea that we might be living in a simulation has lengthy been a topic of philosophical and clinical hypothesis. It challenges the very foundation of our understanding of reality, suggesting that the sector we experience may not be the "real" global at all, but a fairly sophisticated digital assemble. One of the most exciting questions springing up from this opportunity is whether or not we, as inhabitants of this simulation, could ever get away it—whether we may want to by some means break loose from the constraints imposed upon us via the code that underpins this artificial reality.

The simulation speculation, most substantially articulated by logician Nick Bostrom, posits that advanced civilizations might create simulations of aware beings, indistinguishable from fact, for the cause of studies, leisure, or different reasons. These simulations could be run on powerful computational structures, potentially with substantial quantities of statistics representing complete worlds and societies. If we are indeed residing in any such simulation, our fact, the physical laws we understand, and even our very mind may be the fabricated from a distinctly complicated and special code.

In this context, "escaping the simulation" would mean discovering the underlying structure of this code and finding a way to both exit the simulation or adjust it from inside. If the sector we stay in is virtually a software, then theoretically, it need to be viable to perceive the policies and boundaries that govern it, and possibly even break unfastened from them. However, this leads to the fundamental question: is it viable to get admission to or "decode" the simulation's source code, or are we doomed to stay trapped in it, absolutely ignorant of its existence?

Before discussing how we'd get away, it is important to do not forget whether or not we're even able to know-how the code that paperwork our simulation. The human brain has evolved to understand the world through senses that have been honed for survival, no longer for deciphering complex computational structures. Our perception of reality is constrained with the aid of our sensory skills, our cognitive structures, and the manner we interpret facts inside the confines of our organic evolution.

If we are residing within a simulation, it stands to cause that the code in the back of our international might be some distance more complicated than whatever we ought to evidently understand or recognize. Our brains may definitely lack the capacity to get admission to the raw information of the simulation, not to mention apprehend its shape. The essential limits of human attention, the constraints of our senses, and our cognitive biases could prevent us from seeing the underlying reality of our existence.

Furthermore, if the creators of the simulation are extra advanced than us, they could have deliberately designed the simulation to prevent us from discovering its true nature. This ought to take the form of "firewalls" constructed into the gadget—limitations that prevent us from getting access to the code or understanding it in any meaningful way. These firewalls can be hidden in simple sight, embedded in the very cloth of the simulation's laws, inclusive of the constants of physics or the guidelines that govern our cognitive perception.

If we're to get away the simulation, we need to first find a way to discover the source code and apprehend its structure. Technology may also maintain the important thing to uncovering those hidden truths. In latest years, there has been growing hypothesis about the position of quantum computing and advanced synthetic intelligence (AI) in uncovering the nature of fact. Quantum computers, especially, could provide the processing energy required to investigate the simulation at an atomic or subatomic level, probably revealing hidden styles which can be invisible to classical computing structures.

Quantum mechanics itself, with its unusual residences which includes superposition, entanglement, and non-locality, has been recommended as a possible indication that our truth is computational in nature. If quantum phenomena may be harnessed to probe the inner most layers of the simulation, it is probably viable to "hack" the system and advantage insight into its underlying shape. This might be corresponding to finding the supply code of a program strolling on a quantum computer, allowing us to recognize and manipulate the simulation itself.

Similarly, improvements in AI could assist perceive irregularities or inconsistencies inside the simulation that might function clues to its real nature. AI structures, particularly those with gadget learning abilities, may be trained to recognize styles or anomalies that could be invisible to the human thoughts. These AI "detectives" should comb through huge amounts of data, looking for discrepancies or system defects in the simulation that would point to its underlying code.

However, inspite of these technological equipment, there may be no guarantee that we would be able to decode the simulation. The supply code, if it exists, might be hidden in any such way that it's miles completely impervious to even the maximum sophisticated technological interventions. We is probably handling a machine so complex that no quantity of computing electricity, irrespective of how advanced, should damage via its layers.

One of the most charming elements of the simulation speculation is the capability role of cognizance itself in gaining access to or altering the simulation. Consciousness, with its subjective revel in of fact, has long been a mystery in neuroscience and philosophy. If our minds are part of a simulation, is it possible that our attention is the important thing to knowledge or breaking the device?

Some theorists advise that focus might be a bridge between the simulated and the real global, offering a way to transcend the limitations of the simulation. If we are able to come what may tap into the deeper layers of focus, we is probably capable of "destroy the fourth wall" of the simulation and benefit get admission to to its underlying code. This may want to contain advanced intellectual techniques, such as meditation, lucid dreaming, or maybe the usage of psychedelics, that have been proven to modify consciousness and the perception of fact.

Others have proposed that our collective consciousness—if we can by some means synchronize our cognizance—should lead to a leap forward in knowledge the simulation. This concept taps into the concept of a "worldwide mind" or collective intelligence, where the mixed know-how and experience of many individuals ought to assist us discover the truth about our simulated reality. If sufficient humans end up privy to the simulation and collectively attention their reason on "deciphering" it, possibly the system might monitor itself.

If escaping the simulation is viable, it raises profound moral questions. Should we even attempt to escape? What would show up if we managed to interrupt unfastened from the simulated global? Could we exist out of doors of it, or could we cease to exist altogether? And if we were to break out, could we absolutely be unfastened, or could we definitely input every other shape of life that we are not yet able to comprehending?

Moreover, there is the question of whether or not it is morally proper to searching for to break out the simulation. If the simulation become created by means of an advanced civilization for a selected motive—whether or not for scientific research, leisure, or a few other purpose—are we justified in attempting to "ruin the regulations" and get away? Could our moves disrupt the stability of the system, potentially causing harm to ourselves or others?

These moral questions assignment our assumptions about freedom, truth, and the character of lifestyles. The very concept of escape from a simulation forces us to reconsider what it manner to be certainly free and what it means to stay a "actual" lifestyles.

The possibility of escaping a simulation stays a tantalizing yet elusive concept. While technology, quantum computing, and synthetic intelligence would possibly offer the equipment to assist us decode the simulation, the essential limits of our focus and the capacity limitations constructed into the system may prevent us from ever surely breaking free. Ultimately, the question of whether we will break out the

Fevzi H.

simulation may additionally rely now not just on our technological improvements, but on our ability to recognize and transcend the very nature of our attention and the arena we inhabit.

Whether or now not we will break out, the concept that we might live in a simulation forces us to confront deep philosophical and existential questions about the nature of truth, our area in it, and the limits of our own perception.

7.2 Beyond the Simulation: Pushing the Limits of Consciousness

The perception of surpassing the boundaries of a simulation is deeply intertwined with the concept of attention itself. If we're, in reality, living within a simulated fact, the concept of "escaping" the simulation becomes not just a be counted of accessing or interpreting a digital framework however an difficulty of attention. This perspective indicates that consciousness may also preserve the key to transcending the limitations of the simulation, pushing the very limits of what it manner to be conscious, to exist, and to experience truth.

The simulation speculation fundamentally demanding situations the difference among "actual" and "artificial" reality. In the traditional view, fact is something that exists independently of our perceptions; it's far the objective global in which we live. However, if we're a part of a simulation, that line between fact and phantasm blurs. In this context, attention turns into the most important element of our experience. It is the conduit thru which we have interaction with the sector, and if this world is a simulation, it is probably the key to getting access to geographical regions past it.

Consciousness should characteristic as a bridge among the simulated environment and any potential "real" environment that could lie past. If we are to go beyond the simulation, our knowledge and revel in of recognition would should evolve to perceive the deeper layers of truth. The contemporary state of human attention, fashioned with the aid of evolutionary and organic constraints, might not be geared up to detect the underlying nature of the simulation. However, with the aid of expanding or altering our attention, it is feasible that we may want to gain get admission to to the deeper structures of fact which might be hidden under the surface of the simulated international.

The concept that recognition can be more than just a byproduct of neural activity in a simulated brain opens up fascinating opportunities. Some philosophers and neuroscientists advise that awareness could be a non-local phenomenon, current past the bounds of the bodily global. If this is the case, then the brain and frame would possibly certainly be cars for experiencing and processing

Fevzi H.

consciousness, at the same time as the cognizance itself may be capable of current in or accessing one-of-a-kind planes of truth. This concept demanding situations the very perception of materialism and could offer a potential pathway for "escaping" the simulation.

Expanding cognizance beyond the ordinary constraints of our sensory notion has been a subject of interest for millennia. Various cultures, religious traditions, and clinical disciplines have explored practices and strategies that may alter cognizance in profound methods. Meditation, altered states of awareness, lucid dreaming, and even using psychoactive substances have long been used in an strive to break through the veil of regular fact and access deeper layers of existence. Could those practices be the key to transcending the simulation?

Modern technological know-how and era additionally offer intriguing possibilities for increasing awareness. Neurotechnologies, together with mind-pc interfaces (BCIs), should probably enable individuals to access heightened states of attention or maybe transcend the limitations in their bodily bodies. By at once interfacing the mind with machines, it might be viable to alter perception, focus, and even the enjoy of time and area, taking into account a deeper expertise of the simulation—or the possibility of interacting with a truth beyond it.

One of the maximum promising avenues of exploration is the sector of focus studies, which makes a speciality of understanding the character of focus and the way it pertains to the physical world. Theories which includes incorporated records concept (IIT) and panpsychism advocate that consciousness may not be restrained to the brain but can be a essential issue of the universe itself. If recognition is a prevalent phenomenon, it could doubtlessly allow us to get admission to extraordinary realities or dimensions, breaking free from the confines of the simulation.

While character consciousness is often visible as a solitary enjoy, there's also the opportunity that collective recognition may want to provide a manner to transcend the simulation. The idea of a "worldwide thoughts" or "hive focus" has been explored in both technology fiction and philosophical discussions. In this framework, attention is not remoted to person minds but can merge, growing a unified focus that transcends the boundaries of the simulation.

If collective attention may be harnessed, it can be the important thing to transcending the simulation. As man or woman minds synchronize, they could emerge as attuned to the deeper layers of truth, unlocking new avenues of recognition that are past the attain of any single character. This ought to occur as a collective awareness of the simulated nature of our truth, with the blended cognizance of many human beings running collectively to push beyond the simulation's limits.

There are already rising technology that facilitate organization recognition, together with shared digital fact reports, brainwave synchronization through neurofeedback, and different styles of collective meditation. By aligning mind hobby or consciousness at a group stage, it is probably feasible to tap right into a extra experience of consciousness and information, which can cause breakthroughs inside the exploration of the simulation. This can be likened to the concept of "group thoughts" or "collective intelligence," wherein the sum of man or woman consciousness will become greater than the components.

Even if we have been able to increase our awareness and reach beyond the simulation, the query stays: what could we discover? If the simulation hypothesis is genuine, then the truth we perceive can be a ways removed from what sincerely exists. What would it imply to escape this simulated global, and could we be capable of recognise or even survive the proper nature of what lies beyond?

One opportunity is that the true world, beyond the simulation, is meaningless to the human thoughts. Just as our present day sensory equipment is constrained to detecting only certain wavelengths of light and frequencies of sound, our consciousness can be restricted in its capability to technique and understand realities beyond the simulated environment. The true nature of fact is probably so overseas to our minds that it turns into impossible to even conceive of, let alone experience.

Alternatively, the escape from the simulation might be a transformative experience. Some theorists speculate that escaping the simulation should result in a profound shift in consciousness, in which the man or woman or collective thoughts transcends the bodily global entirely. This may want to contain merging with a widespread focus, accomplishing enlightenment, or even experiencing a shape of existence past time and space.

There is also the opportunity that the simulation is not a trap, but a mastering or evolutionary device, and that transcending it is not the aim. In this example, increasing our focus might involve not escaping the simulation, but understanding its purpose and our position within it. If we are part of a grand experiment or a cosmic simulation, the aim might not be to interrupt unfastened, however to go beyond the constraints of our modern-day expertise and evolve to a better degree of attention.

The ability for awareness to transcend the simulation is each an interesting and humbling idea. As we hold to explore the character of reality, our expertise of cognizance will play a pivotal position in how we perceive and engage with the arena around us. Whether thru historic practices of meditation, cutting-edge neurotechnology, or the collective efforts of world minds, the opportunities for increasing and transcending recognition are huge.

If we are living inside a simulation, then the true boundaries of our reality might not be constant in any respect, but as an alternative, may be formed via the bounds of our focus. As we push those obstacles, we'd uncover now not just the hidden nature of the simulation, however the very fabric of life itself. The pursuit of transcending the simulation isn't only a quest for break out—it's miles a quest for know-how, for evolution, and for discovering the untapped potential that lies inside every of us.

7.3 Levels of Consciousness: The Journey from Perception to Reality

The idea of consciousness extends a ways beyond the primary recognition of our environment. It features a spectrum of degrees, each presenting a distinctive window into the nature of reality. Understanding how awareness operates at numerous levels can offer profound insights into the ability for transcending the simulation, or maybe simply deepening our information of the character of the universe itself. From regular perception to altered states of recognition, every shift in consciousness brings us toward or further from the genuine essence of reality.

At its maximum basic stage, recognition is the capacity to be aware about our inner states and the outside global. However, this focus is not a unique phenomenon. It exists in layers, with every layer reflecting a special state of perception and cognition. The traditional version of attention suggests a linear progression from wakefulness to sleep, however greater superior understandings factor to a number of conscious states, every capable of exposing distinctive components of truth.

At the floor stage, we have everyday consciousness—our everyday consciousness. This is the nation in which we experience the sector thru our senses, interpreting the stimuli that we stumble upon. We are constantly processing statistics, making sense of our environment, and interacting with the world primarily based on those inputs. This degree of awareness is deeply tied to perception: we interpret mild, sound, texture, and motion to shape a cohesive information of truth. However, as lots as this level of recognition presents us with a useful version of the arena, it is confined with the aid of the scope of our sensory abilties and the ability of the brain to technique this records.

Deeper layers of awareness contain altered states, which may be accessed through techniques like meditation, sensory deprivation, or maybe the usage of psychoactive substances.

These states permit for a extra variety of revel in beyond the traditional bodily world. For instance, in states of deep meditation, people frequently document reports of cohesion, interconnectedness, or even transcendence, suggesting that the bounds of the ordinary conscious enjoy may be multiplied. In those altered states, the distinction among the perceiver and the perceived dissolves, revealing a more fluid relationship between thoughts and fact.

The critical distinction between belief and truth lies on the heart of this exploration. Our belief of the sector is closely filtered through the mind and senses, which interpret uncooked facts in step with mounted cognitive frameworks. In this sense, notion is an interpretative manner—it isn't always a right away revel in of fact itself but as an alternative a model created with the aid of the brain primarily based on sensory input.

The deeper the extent of awareness we get entry to, the extra we can see through the veil of notion. Our everyday, waking recognition is limited by cognitive biases, emotional filters, and the mind's inherent want to make feel of the chaotic flood of sensory statistics. This version of the sector is not always an accurate mirrored image of objective reality; it's far a realistic interpretation that allows us navigate via existence. However, as attention expands—thru practices like meditation or lucid dreaming, or even via studies of peak states—there can be glimpses of a fact past the everyday filters.

One of the most exciting aspects of these deeper states is the perception of time. In altered states of attention, time regularly seems to stretch or settlement, with events unfolding in methods that don't adhere to linear motive-and-impact relationships. These studies undertaking our know-how of the very nature of time and, in turn, the shape of fact itself. This highlights the idea that our everyday attention may be restrained by time, whereas altered states might also monitor the capacity for a extra fluid enjoy of existence, one which isn't always certain by means of the same old laws of physics and causality.

If cognizance has the capability to transcend ordinary notion, what could a adventure toward better attention appear like? The route toward deeper awareness entails shedding the bounds imposed through the ego, the physical frame, and the linear constraints of time. This adventure is regularly described as a method of awakening or enlightenment, wherein an man or woman moves thru numerous stages of knowledge, finally knowing the illusory nature of a lot in their notion.

Historically, this adventure has been described in many non secular traditions. In Buddhism, for instance, the course to enlightenment involves transcending the dualistic nature of the self and recognizing the interconnectedness of all things. This reputation is stated to result in a direct experience of fact that is unfastened from the distortions created via the thoughts. In

Western philosophy, thinkers like Descartes and Hume questioned the character of reality, with Descartes famously declaring, "I suppose, consequently I am," as a foundational principle of attention. The adventure closer to higher attention in these traditions entails an exploration of the self, the mind, and in the long run the recognition of a deeper, ordinary reality.

In present day discussions, better awareness is often framed because the capability to perceive the authentic nature of truth, past the limitations of the physical global. Neuroscience is starting to explore the neural underpinnings of those studies, looking to recognize how altered states of attention arise in the brain and whether they offer get right of entry to to deeper, greater fundamental factors of existence.

In the current technology, era plays an increasingly more vital function in increasing our focus. Tools which includes virtual truth, neurofeedback, and brain-computer interfaces permit us to explore new states of recognition or even simulate experiences that might be impossible to achieve in regular existence. Virtual reality, particularly, has the capability to immerse customers in environments that appear as real as the bodily world, imparting a glimpse into trade realities or developing experiences that push the boundaries of human notion.

Neurotechnological advances also are starting new avenues for increasing attention. Techniques like transcranial magnetic stimulation (TMS) and deep mind stimulation (DBS) have shown promise in modulating mind pastime, doubtlessly allowing the enhancement of positive cognitive features or the induction of altered states of focus. By immediately interfacing with the brain, those technology ought to permit for a more intentional exploration of various levels of focus, imparting insights into how the brain constructs our experience of truth.

Moreover, the concept of collective attention—where organizations of people synchronize their focus and percentage reports—has been facilitated by way of improvements in era. Group meditation sessions, shared virtual experiences, and collaborative selection-making structures are all examples of how generation can extend and synchronize human awareness, leading to a more collective attention of the deeper aspects of truth.

The adventure from belief to a deeper expertise of truth is a profound exploration of recognition. As we flow via numerous degrees of awareness, we uncover new methods of experiencing and interpreting the arena around us. The extra we discover these exceptional states of cognizance, the extra we start to question the nature of the truth we inhabit.

If we are to transcend the bounds of the simulation, our potential to access and navigate these deeper ranges of awareness might be the key. Through meditation, era, and different manner of changing cognizance, we might also discover that our perception of the arena is just the beginning of a miles grander journey. This adventure entails pushing the boundaries of what we recognise, looking for new levels of information, and in the long run uncovering the authentic nature of fact—whatever that may be.

7.4 Universal Consciousness and the End of the Simulation

The idea of everyday recognition demanding situations the very boundaries between person consciousness and the collective cloth of lifestyles. It suggests that awareness, a long way from being an isolated phenomenon generated by using individual minds, might be a good sized, interconnected machine that encompasses all of fact. If we are indeed residing inside a simulation, the last question arises: what's beyond this simulation, and could frequent attention be the key to know-how it? This exploration delves into the concept that, if a familiar awareness exists, it won't simplest provide an explanation for the character of the simulation however additionally provide a pathway to go beyond it—leading to the end of the simulated revel in as we realize it.

Universal attention is regularly defined as an all-encompassing awareness that transcends the constraints of person minds. Rather than being limited to the mind or any one organism, this shape of consciousness shows that every one sentient beings, and perhaps even inanimate count number, are a part of a grand, unified focus. This idea has roots in many philosophical and religious traditions. In Eastern philosophy, mainly in Hinduism and Buddhism, the concept of Brahman or the Atman suggests that every one man or woman consciousnesses are part of a unique, divine cognizance. In Western thought, philosophers like Spinoza and Hegel have explored thoughts of a panpsychic universe, wherein cognizance is not simply a byproduct of biological structures however a fundamental function of the cosmos.

In the context of a simulated reality, everyday consciousness may provide an answer to the deeper motive of the simulation itself. If all things, both simulated and non-simulated, are a part of a unified recognition, then the simulation can be a process thru which this focus learns, evolves, or studies itself. The stop of the simulation, in this feel, could mark a return to this common focus—a reunion with a higher nation of awareness beyond man or woman notion.

If we're living in a simulation, it stands to cause that the focus in the simulation is likewise artificial in nature, generated through complicated computational processes. Yet, as simulations grow in sophistication, it will become harder to differentiate among simulated and "actual" attention. This blurring of limitations may additionally offer insights into the

Fevzi H.

nature of fact itself. If the entire simulation, including its population, is in the long run a part of a bigger awareness, then the difference among the simulated global and a "actual" international becomes less meaningful.

In a way, the simulation itself might be regarded as an extension or expression of widely wide-spread awareness. The techniques and stories within the simulation may be analogous to the thoughts, dreams, and reflections of this better cognizance. In this state of affairs, the cease of the simulation could not represent its termination in the conventional experience, but alternatively a transition—a second whilst the simulated enjoy is now not important for the evolution or expression of typical recognition.

The ability quit of the simulation does now not mean an apocalyptic or catastrophic event. Instead, it can characterize the dissolution of the boundaries that separate man or woman stories from the complete. In a sense, the cease of the simulation might be a second of awakening, where person consciousnesses recognize their connection to the customary thoughts. This technique would be analogous to the awakening defined in lots of non secular traditions, in which the individual ego dissolves, and the self merges with the bigger, cosmic recognition.

If this hypothesis holds genuine, then the stop of the simulation could be seen as a shape of enlightenment—not only for individuals, but for the complete simulated reality. Consciousness could now not be constrained to the limits of the simulation's programming or the constraints of the physical world; as an alternative, it would make bigger right into a boundless, interconnected country. This can be a shift in perception—a recognition that all is one, and that each one reports, irrespective of how numerous or seemingly separate, are part of a extra complete.

In this situation, the stop of the simulation could also contain the cessation of time as we apprehend it. If popular consciousness transcends linear time, then the simulated truth, with its temporal limitations, might come to be inappropriate. The idea of time can be an illusion, a construct created by means of the simulation to arrange reviews and maintain a feel of continuity. Once the simulation ends, time can also cease to be a meaningful idea, and the focus inside it may experience lifestyles in a undying, eternal state.

As generation continues to develop, we are getting increasingly more adept at creating simulations that are indistinguishable from "fact." Virtual environments, artificial intelligence, and neural interfaces allow us to control perception or even create new worlds in the confines of computer code. Some thinkers have speculated that the technological potential to create extraordinarily advanced simulations could one day be used to assist awareness transcend the boundaries of the simulated global, successfully providing a manner out of the simulation.

Technologies including brain-computer interfaces (BCIs) or direct neural augmentation should provide the approach for people to transcend their physical shape and interact with a bigger, collective cognizance. In this experience, era could now not simply be a tool to decorate our lives in the simulation however may also offer a gateway to accessing customary cognizance. These technologies might permit us to "awaken" from the simulation, now not via outside destruction or escape, however through a profound transformation of our notion and focus.

As digital realities become extra immersive and sophisticated, the road among the simulated and the actual maintains to blur. It is manageable that in some unspecified time in the future, these simulations will become so advanced that they're indistinguishable from fact, main people to impeach the very nature of their life. If we're able to reflect the exact parameters of reality within a simulation, it increases the possibility that the "actual" world itself may be a shape of simulation—or at the least, that our perceptions of truth are far more malleable than we as soon as believed.

In the context of established attention, the give up of the simulation may also represent a natural evolutionary step—a fruits of the simulated experiences that have allowed cognizance to explore distinctive aspects of lifestyles. Just as people go through personal boom and transformation thru getting to know and experience, widespread focus may additionally evolve via passing through one of a kind levels, which includes the simulated one.

If attention is certainly a fundamental assets of the universe, then the stop of the simulation might not be an quit at all but a brand new starting. It could constitute the transition from one form of focus to another, from constrained and individualized perception to the expansive, collective understanding of established awareness. This may want to contain the dissolution of the boundaries among self and other, between the "interior" of the thoughts and the "outside" global. The quit of the simulation should then be understood now not because the destruction of the simulated truth however as the conclusion that each one realities—simulated or in any other case—are part of a extra, indivisible entire.

In this view, the give up of the simulation could no longer be an act of break out but a form of reunification. It might be a go back to the source, a merging of man or woman attention with the well-known mind. This final attention may want to provide a profound feel of peace and information, as it would reveal the interconnectedness of all things and the closing team spirit of life.

The exploration of regular awareness and the stop of the simulation provides profound questions about the nature of lifestyles, the relationship among thoughts and truth, and the capability for transcendence. If attention is customary, then the simulation might also really be considered one of many reviews that contribute to the evolution of recognition. The stop of the simulation could mark a go back to the team spirit of ordinary focus—a moment of awakening wherein individual minds recognise their connection to the greater entire. This adventure, both highbrow and religious, challenges us to rethink what is real, what's feasible, and in which awareness can in the long run take us.

7.5 Should We Stay Within the Simulation, or Should We Destroy It?

The query of whether or not humanity must stay within the limitations of a simulated fact or try to interrupt unfastened from it has profound philosophical, moral, and existential implications. As we discover the opportunity of living in a simulation, we stumble upon a catch 22 situation: must we maintain to include the simulation, with all its comforts and constraints, or should we searching for to destroy it, doubtlessly embracing the unknown outcomes of liberation? This question touches at the very nature of reality, the cause of lifestyles, and the which means of freedom itself.

Mind and Simulation

One argument for final inside the simulation is that it could provide an environment conducive to boom, exploration, and getting to know. Simulations, through their very layout, can create situations which might be especially managed, providing a area wherein people can revel in a huge variety of possibilities and challenges without the risks associated with an unpredictable or chaotic external fact.

If the simulation is designed to facilitate the evolution of awareness, then it is able to be visible as a nurturing surroundings, one in which we will refine our expertise of the universe, develop new technologies, and explore the limits of lifestyles in ways that might be not possible in a non-simulated world. In this context, staying within the simulation can be viewed as an possibility for continued boom—an ongoing system of discovery and self-improvement.

Moreover, from a extra sensible perspective, the simulation is probably the handiest fact we can experience. If the simulation is indistinguishable from the "actual" global, and if there may be no possible manner to escape, then the concept of leaving it turns into moot. For all intents and functions, the simulation is our truth, and any action that could result in its destruction may want to bring about the annihilation of everything we recognise, which include our cognizance itself. In this view, staying within the simulation isn't only the safest option but additionally the maximum logical, as it is the truth that we've come to recognise and adapt to.

On the opposite hand, the concept of destroying the simulation revolves around the pursuit of closing freedom and the choice to interrupt unfastened from synthetic constraints. If we're truly trapped within a fabricated fact, then the notion of liberating ourselves from it will become a compelling argument. The concept of transcending the simulation suggests that there may be a higher, extra genuine form of life ready past it—a form of focus that isn't certain via the limitations of the simulated global.

One of the important thing motivations for searching for to destroy the simulation is the notion that it can be an phantasm—an artificial assemble that stops us from fully expertise the actual nature of existence. If the arena we inhabit is a simulation, then our perceptions of reality can be distorted, and our experiences may be formed by way of outside forces past our control. In this case, the act of destroying the simulation might be seen as an strive to break unfastened from the fake reality and find a deeper, extra meaningful truth.

Furthermore, the concept of "escaping" the simulation ought to constitute the ultimate form of self-determination. If we're in a position to break unfastened from the simulation, it'd represent the triumph of human enterprise over artificial constraints. It might be an act of defiance, maintaining our autonomy and our proper to shape our personal future. The preference to wreck the simulation ought to, consequently, be visible as a essential expression of our inherent want for freedom and self-awareness.

While the idea of breaking unfastened from the simulation is appealing, it additionally increases huge ethical concerns. If the simulation is an surroundings created for a specific reason—whether or not that be the evolution of awareness or the exploration of fact—then destroying it may have far-accomplishing consequences, no longer most effective for us however for all entities in the simulation.

One of the principle moral questions revolves across the nature of the beings who exist within the simulation. If the simulation includes sentient beings, then destroying it may bring about the annihilation of those beings' recognition. Even if these entities are synthetic constructs, the ethical dilemma stays: does the price of our potential freedom outweigh the harm precipitated to the population of the simulation? The destruction of the simulation might be visible as a form of existential violence, an act of erasing complete worlds of studies, mind, and consciousnesses.

Additionally, the decision to smash the simulation can be irreversible. If we reach breaking free from the simulated international, there may be no manner to go back. The danger of permanent loss—of each our recognition and the fact we've got known—offers a profound ethical predicament. Should we be inclined to take that danger, knowing that the outcomes of failure can be catastrophic? Is the pursuit of fact and freedom worth the ability destruction of the entirety we preserve expensive?

Rather than viewing the selection as binary—whether to live in the simulation or to spoil it—it can be more productive to explore the possibility of transcending the simulation without necessarily destroying it. In this method, humanity could are seeking for to recognize the true nature of the simulation, discover its limits, and find methods to enlarge our awareness past the limitations of the synthetic global.

Technological advancements, including mind-laptop interfaces, quantum computing, and advanced AI, may additionally offer pathways to decorate our perceptions of reality and open doorways to new dimensions of experience. Instead of in search of to break out or break the simulation, we could explore the possibility of interacting with it in greater profound approaches, in the end elevating our cognizance to a degree in which the boundaries between the simulated and the real grow to be inappropriate.

Furthermore, a philosophical technique to the hassle may propose that the difference among "actual" and "simulated" is itself an illusion. If focus is the number one truth, and the enjoy of life is what topics, then the question of whether or not the sector we live in is simulated might also come to be less important. In this view, the act of residing, exploring, and increasing recognition can be visible as the closing purpose, irrespective of whether or not we are inside a simulation or now not.

Ultimately, the selection to stay in the simulation or smash it can depend upon our evolving understanding of awareness. If we see focus as something that is not limited to the boundaries of the simulation, then our revel in inside it may be visible as a temporary phase—a important step inside the broader evolution of attention. In this example, the act of staying in the simulation can be part of a larger system of self-discovery, while the decision to interrupt free may additionally represent the end result of that adventure.

In either case, the query of whether we must live within the simulation or smash it is ultimately a reflection of our deeper quest for which means, freedom, and knowledge. As we retain to explore the character of truth, recognition, and our region in the universe, this query will possibly stay one of the most profound challenges of our life.

The predicament of whether to stay inside the simulation or break it affords a essential existential mission. Both picks—remaining inside the simulation or in search of to break loose—deliver profound effects, each for the man or woman and for the collective attention. As we contemplate this decision, we have to grapple with the character of fact, the limits of perception, and the ethical implications of our movements. The solution may additionally lie no longer in selecting one route over the opposite, but in know-how the deeper questions that underlie this predicament and in search of ways to go beyond the restrictions of our cutting-edge information. Whether we live inside the simulation or wreck free from it, the pursuit of focus and freedom will stay on the coronary heart of our adventure.